HOLLYWOOD WINGMAN

Hanging Out with Mavericks, Moguls and Maniacs in LA Show Biz and Lakers Showtime

Joe Bucz

CENTRAL PARK SOUTH PUBLISHING

Published by Central Park South Publishing 2022
www.centralparksouthpublishing.com

Typesetting and e-book formatting services by Victor Marcos

ISBN:
978-1-956452-13-6 (pbk)
978-1-956452-14-3 (hbk)
978-1-956452-15-0 (ebk)

This book is dedicated to a pair of Bruces, one my blood brother, the other my surrogate brother—Bruce Bucz *and* Bruce Paltrow

CONTENTS

Chapter 1

⎯⎯⎯⎯∞∞∞⎯⎯⎯⎯

WARREN BEATTY AS... ROLE MODEL?

It is 2008, and I am sitting at my computer as an Account Executive for the Los Angeles Sparks women's basketball team (Account Executive being a fancy title for salesman, as Charlie Sheen found out in the film *Wall Street*), when an e-mail pops up on my screen. It reads:

"Joe. Trying to find you. The number I have no longer works. If you get this, respond. Got an idea you might be interested in? Hope all is well.—MH"

My heart literally skipped a beat, as I knew that MH stood for Mark Harmon, the then and current star of one of the most successful TV series in history, NCIS. What was Mark Harmon doing e-mailing a salesperson for the WNBA? Well, it was not to buy tickets, and the story begins back in the late 1960's Chicago suburb of Willow Springs, the same town where the Keanu Reeves and Sandra Bullock movie *The Lake House* was shot, but more on Keanu later.

Remember the old disingenuous expression about just reading *Playboy* for the "interesting articles?" Growing up in Willow Springs, I was quite the voracious reader: first comic books and then, for some unknown, cosmic, twist of fate reason, during my teens I started reading *Esquire* magazine. Don't get me wrong, I not only read *Playboy* as well, but also the more scandalous *Oui* magazine, which "showed more" and in one particular issue, featured a British bombshell named Fiona, more on her later also. At the time, *Esquire* featured extremely literate profiles of movie stars, and the articles really captured my imagination—the first one to really get my attention was by the well-known New York critic and media gadfly Rex Reed and was called "Will the Real Warren Beatty Please Shut Up." (Reed's colorful, insulting prose style would have made Simon Cowell blush).

At the time, I was a sophomore in high school, and three incredibly influential films were released in the last three consecutive years—*Bonnie and Clyde* in 1967, *Bullitt* starring Steve McQueen in 1968 and the first pairing of Robert Redford and Paul Newman in *Butch Cassidy and the Sundance Kid* in 1969. The second pairing of them would change my life forever, but more on that later. I was vaguely aware that Beatty had been the force behind the pop culture movie phenomenon *Bonnie and Clyde*, and Reed's article made him out to be a callow ladies' man and male diva. Nevertheless, I was enthralled by the concept of a major movie star who did not partake of the usual vices of the time of smoking, drinking, and drugs, but rather focused all of his intellectual ability on all aspects of filmmaking and compartmentalized his social life to wooing and bedding every leading lady in and out of Hollywood. To a shy small-town kid like myself, this sounded about as glamorous a life as was possible to lead! At the time, Beatty was receiving begrudging recognition from the New York media for not giving up on the initial commercial box office failure of *Bonnie*, but rather, armed with some glowing reviews from some influential critics in New York, launched a re-release campaign with Warner Brothers. This generated the publicity about the film's controversial statement on the realistic portrayal of violence in film and its carry over effect on the country's increasing intolerance for the ongoing war in Vietnam.

This would be neatly summarized in a book about the film, which featured photos by a photographer named Curtis Hanson, and disclosed the nugget that the script underwent a rewrite by a then unknown screenwriter named Robert Towne.

This would also foreshadow Beatty's future entry into the political arena, which brings us to Southern Illinois University at Carbondale in 1972. I was adrift, after a short stint on the football team, with the vague notion that if I really wanted to be an actor, I should quit college, as Beatty did, and go to New York to study acting under the same world-renowned acting teacher, Stella Adler. As fate would have it, I decided to join the on-campus campaign to elect George McGovern for President, and who should happen to be coming to our modest campus to stump on McGovern's behalf but one Mr. Warren Beatty! Having been on the football team, I immediately volunteered to be Beatty's "bodyguard" during his appearance, which of course was an excuse on my part to get up close and personal with my legendary acting idol. My mind raced with a million different questions that I would ask him if given the chance, but when the moment arrived, all I could manage was "I saw McCabe & Mrs. Miller seven times," to which he replied "Jesus Christ," and that was that. I did manage, however, to get close enough to him to pose for pictures while waiting for him to go onstage, and I must give myself credit for that—looking at the pictures, I was standing so close to Beatty that you would have thought that I was McGovern's campaign manager, Gary Hart. Hart also took Beatty's womanizing to "heart," which would come back to bite him during his own political campaign years later. At any rate, just being in the presence of my acting idol was inspiration enough to plant the seed in my mind that I should go to New York or LA to attend acting school. One of my professors at the time advised me to quit school immediately and go to New York, but my mother was determined that I get my college degree, so I did graduate from SIU with a degree in film. Ironically, I did make the Dean's list one quarter, which was helped in no small part due to a term paper I wrote on *Bonnie and Clyde* and the realistic portrayal of violence. I also wrote a film review of *The Candidate*, starring my other favorite actor, Robert Redford, which was published in the student newspaper, so I felt like I was the top film student at SIU. I tried to emulate my idol Beatty by playing a scene from one of his early stage roles, *A Loss of Roses* by William Inge, directed by a talented grad school director named Joe Nunley. Little did I realize at the time that mine and Joe's path would cross again in a couple of years. I also left with fond memories of my own on campus sexual liaisons inspired by Beatty's womanizing, but more a result of the general overall sexual freedom of the 70's "free love generation" and SIU's reputation as the number one party school in the country according to, yes, *Playboy* magazine.

As luck and fate would have it, one of my college friends, Mike Pullis, received a job offer in Los Angeles immediately upon graduation, so after a summer of working in Chicago to try and save a little money, I arranged to drive out to California and join Mike in his temporary apartment in Burbank. A city made dubiously famous at the time by Johnny Carson's sarcastic refence on his show of "beautiful downtown Burbank." To me, a young hick from the Midwest, Burbank was indeed truly beautiful, as Mike's apartment was on Riverside Drive. It was right down the street from the Burbank Studios, which at the time housed both Columbia Pictures and Warner Brothers, the studio which released and then successfully re-released *Bonnie and Clyde*—I was becoming a big believer in fate at a relatively young age! Now that my dream factory of studios was right down the street from me, I did want to go to acting school and try and pursue a career, but the hard reality of making a living while doing so was also staring me in the face. What to do?

Of course! Call my "old buddy" Warren Beatty and ask him for his advice! As ridiculous as that notion sounds, I was at least realistic enough to realize that I had to try and contact Beatty through his agent. I was literally able to give it the old college try—Mike's friend, a makeup man in the movie business, found out for me that he was represented by Stan Kamen of the William Morris Agency, which at the time was known as the number one talent agency in the world. Remember, this is 1973, before the Ari Golds of the Entourage world had cell phones or even answering machines, so the only way to get through to an agent was to call their secretaries (the dreaded "gatekeepers") or, if the agent was big enough, his or her assistant/agent trainee. Kamen was so big that he was the only agent at William Morris to have both a secretary AND an assistant, and the rest of my life would be determined by the fact that Kamen's assistant at the time would be a young man named Jim Canchola. Instead of scoffing at my ridiculous request to speak to the hottest movie star in the world, as most assistants would have, he calmly replied that he would pass my message along to Mr. Kamen and that they would get back to me. Anybody with half a brain would have realized that they were receiving the politest of brush offs, but I had the cock-eyed optimism of the most naïve of the naïve, so I sat back and waited with my hands literally folded together in a combination of prayer and anticipation.

My prayers were answered—a couple of days later, Jim called back and said that he had Mr. Kamen on the line! Once again, instead of scolding me for wasting everybody's time, Stan politely told me that "Warren" was out of town in Santa Barbara but that they would relay my message to him when he returned! Dumbfounded that I received any kind of response, I thanked Stan profusely and was on cloud nine the rest of the day. The next day, Jim called back to see how the call had gone, and I thanked him profusely as well. Then he dropped the bombshell—he and Stan had been impressed by my initiative, and they wanted to see if I would be interested in interviewing for a job in the mailroom! I would later learn that every employee at William Morris who had ambitions to be an agent started out in the mail room so that they could literally learn the business from the bottom up. Thus, a position in the William Morris mail room was considered the most desirable entry level position in show business. This opportunity was too good to be true—I was being offered the chance to interview for the same agency that represented not only my idol, Warren Beatty, but also literally hundreds of other actors, directors, writers and producers, most of whom were some of the biggest names in show business! Once I caught my breath, I anxiously agreed, and before I knew it, I was interviewing with their personnel director. He explained to me how their agent trainee program worked—you start in the mailroom for a few months, then you are promoted to dispatch, which was basically an in-house delivery system that hand delivered scripts, contracts and checks to their clients, for a few more months. If you survived that phase, you would then be assigned a "desk," where you would function as a secretary/assistant for one of the agents and learn the finer points of becoming an agent. Before my head could stop spinning, I was hired, and I drove back from their Beverly Hills office to my motel room in Burbank to give my roommate Mike the good news that I would now be able to start kicking in some money for the rent.

Although the mailroom job was as menial as it sounds, it truly was educational because the William Morris motto was "Put it in Writing," so by reading all the memos before you distributed them into the mailboxes, you really did get a sense of the business of the business. There was also no doubt that the office was an exciting place to be, as many clients had to visit the office for various types of meetings, so it would not be unusual to run into a young Robert De Niro in the elevator ("loved you in *Bang the Drum Slowly!*") or happen upon Robert Wagner walking down the sidewalk. The one actor who always made a point of stopping by the mailroom to say hi to me was best known for the beer commercials that I had seen him in back in Chicago, but he was a rising young star with a deep growling voice—Sam Elliott. Little did Sam know at the time that by making a young trainee's day by saying hello that it would come back to help him a few years later.

By this time, I had become very friendly with the young man responsible for giving me the biggest break of my life, Stan's assistant Jim, and I was impressed to find out that Stan was one of the two most powerful actors' agents in Hollywood (the other being Freddie Fields from rival agency CMA, later to become ICM). Stan had represented such icons as Marlon Brando and Steve McQueen, and who currently represented, in addition to Beatty, other big stars like James Caan, Jon Voight, Richard Harris and Kris Kristofferson. I also learned that one of the agent's assistant's duties was to read scripts for their clients, and

Stan represented so many clients that Jim needed help to read them all. He recruited me to give him a hand in "covering" them, which essentially meant writing a book report style synopsis and opinion on each script to see if it would be right for any of the agencies' clients. Being the previously mentioned voracious reader of *Esquire* and comic books, I attacked the task with relish and was excited that my opinion would be taken into consideration by the powers that be. My work could prove to be a knack that would help me climb the ladder on the way to becoming an agent.

By this time, I was also heartened that I was making friends with most of the other trainees, because although it was competitive, there was also a boot camp mentality that we were all in it together. I distinctly remember a group of us all going down to a funky nightclub in Venice to check out a new band that we had heard about. Little did we know that we were witnessing rock music history—the band turned out to be Oingo Boingo, and they and their leader, Danny Elfman, went on to become enormously popular. I became particularly good friends with another fellow trainee, Bruce Brown, and I really lucked out because although he had grown up in a Beverly Hills lifestyle, he was not a "brat," but rather was raised to be a down to earth guy by his powerful but ethical father. Bruce really took me under his wing and initiated me into almost all of the landmark social aspects of Los Angeles, from Musso & Frank's Grill, the Pantry and Apple Pan restaurants, to the card rooms of Gardena, the nightclubs of Hollywood and even the famous and private Playboy Club. Another trainee I became friends with was Vaughn Hart, a good natured and good-hearted guy who took in stride the jokes he received due to the fact that he bore a startling resemblance to Woody Allen. Bruce, Vaughn, and I spent a lot of time hanging out together during off work hours.

One particularly colorful part of my life at that point was the fact that I had become a doorman/bouncer for the most popular nightclub in the San Fernando Valley, The Point After, as I needed to moonlight to supplement the low paying salary of the mailroom. The club was so popular that even the HR guy at William Morris who hired me frequented the club with another Morris employee! It was fun while it lasted, but after I was arrested in the aftermath of a huge brawl (I was not charged), I decided that I had better maintain a lower profile if I were to become a respectable agent, so I turned in my red bouncer jacket. Before I did, however, I was able to take advantage of my position at the club to ask out one of the full-figured customers there, and I had a plan. Jim had told me that Warren Beatty's favorite restaurant at that time was the Aware Inn, a health food restaurant on Sunset Boulevard, and Jim saw nothing wrong with going there as a customer and introducing myself to Beatty if he happened to be dining there one night. Knowing Beatty's penchant for womanizing, I felt that my chances for being well received by him were better if I were in the company of my large bosomed new friend, so we gave it a try!

As luck would have it, Beatty was there with a female companion, and fueled by the fearlessness of youth, I approached his table with my date and told him that I was the one who had left a message for him through Stan seeking his advice on pursuing an acting career. Knowing that he had attended Stella Adler's acting school, I asked him if he would recommend her course, and, giving my date and me the once over, he slyly remarked, "Yeah, she's good with good looking young guys." Surprised and flattered by his mutually complementary remark, I decided not to press my luck and try to exit gracefully. Suffice to say that my date was impressed by this Hollywood moment, and once again, I was dumbfounded that I had been able to converse with my idol. The next day Jim was amused by my anecdote, and I'm sure that he and Warren had a good chuckle over my chutzpah—maybe I did have what it took to become an agent!

By this time, I had been promoted to the dispatch phase of the training, and during one of my more memorable delivery runs, I encountered Paul Newman on the back lot of Fox Studios. He was in the process of filming *Towering Inferno*, and star struck guy that I was, I couldn't help but ask him for his autograph with the excuse of asking for my mother. Unaware of his reputation for turning down autograph seekers, I was devastated when he refused, giving the reason that signing autographs was "bullshit elitism." Seeing how crestfallen I was, he told me to tell my mom that he would buy her a beer, so at least I was able to walk away on a light note. I later read that he really did not give autographs for that reason, that he did not think that he was better than anyone else, and just wanted to be one of the good ol' boys who drank beer and tinkered with cars. In a way, I was glad that it happened, as I had to tone down my reverence for stars and start preparing for a career of representing them. Moreover, I rationalized that the fact that he turned me down made for a better story anyway!

After quite a few months of paying my dues on these delivery runs, I came to find out that they always picked the most promising trainee to become the head of dispatch, so I was excited when I was selected for that position as well. It also meant dealing with the HR assistant, Kathy Krugel, on a daily basis, and she was an amusing combination of part cougar, part politician and total nervous wreck, but we hit it off and developed a rapport of friendly mutual respect. In addition, no description of being an employee of William Morris at that time would be complete without mentioning another employee, one Barbra Bell, an absolutely stunning young woman who was also, not coincidentally, notorious for wearing the sexiest outfits of that time. This normally would have been frowned upon in such a conservative company were it not for the fact that she was the object of every male employee's fantasy desire (think Joan from *Mad Men* without the sexual politics). Barbara was also one of the coolest people you could ever meet, and she became extremely deft at fending off the advances of every would-be suitor in a way that left your ego intact. Being in the orbit of my womanizing idol Beatty, I developed the confidence to try my luck with her, and she did a wonderful job of letting me down as easy as everybody else, for which I will always be grateful. Of all the people I have met over the years, she is one person I would be curious to find out about how her life turned out, because she deserved a happy one.

There was also another secretary employed there who was notorious for a different reason—Michelle Marvin, who became famous for suing her live-in partner, actor Lee Marvin, and thus created the concept of "palimony" lawsuits whereby males could be held financially liable even if the partners were unmarried. Let us just say that I could not blame Lee, Ms. Marvin did not have the sunniest of dispositions, but I must give her credit for her foresight into the future of sexual relationships in society—it was a groundbreaking legal decision.

By this time, it would now not be long before I would be considered for the final phase of the program, getting a desk, and I started to handicap my opportunities. There was no doubt that I wanted to follow in the footsteps of Jim and Stan Kamen as a motion picture agent, but it became apparent that it was going to be awhile before Jim were to become an agent himself, so it looked like I would have to set my sights on another agent to train me. Meanwhile, Jim took a couple of steps to reward me for my dedicated script reading—first, he tipped me off that Beatty was going to be shooting some night scenes in Beverly Hills of his new movie, a fictionalized comedy drama. It was based on some real-life Beverly Hills hairdressers, including the late Jay Sebring, who along with movie star Sharon Tate was viciously murdered by the serial killer and cult leader Charles Manson and his "family," which Quentin Tarantino fictionalized in his film *Once Upon a Time in Hollywood.* Jon Peters, the then current hairdresser of the stars, was also one of the inspirations for Beatty's film, and his legendary temper was amusingly portrayed by Bradley Cooper in the Paul Thomas Anderson film *Licorice Pizza.* I sauntered onto the set that night and tried to look like I belonged, and nobody thought to question me for quite a while until almost the end of the shoot, whereby I mumbled something to the effect that I worked with Beatty's agent's assistant. I have to admit that I was thrilled to see my idol in action and marveled at how far I had come since we were standing together in Carbondale.

Then, a couple of months later, the film was ready to be shown in a rough-cut screening, and Jim surprised me by inviting me to go with him to the screening. It was shown in a small screening room at Paramount, and there was no doubt that it was an exclusive audience handpicked by Beatty to give him feedback on the film. Once again, I could not believe my good fortune that I was a small part of movie history, as the film, *Shampoo*, turned out to be a huge hit for its satirical take on the combination of sexual and real politics. Jim made a point of introducing me to Beatty on the way out of the screening, and, as I complemented the film as enthusiastically as I could, I could not help but feel that I was on top of the world. Little did I know at that moment another cast member of that movie would have the biggest impact on me of anybody in my lifetime, but first, it was time for me to get my own desk at William Morris and start learning to become a bona fide agent!

There was also another client of Kamen who was featured in Tarantino's film, but I doubt that many people know why. There is a shot of the cowboy actor James Stacy, played by Timothy Olyphant, leaving the set of the TV show Lancer on a motorcycle, and it is significant. The real James Stacy was involved in a motorcycle accident which killed his girlfriend and left him without a left arm and leg. Kamen arranged with another one of his clients, Kirk Douglas, to write Stacy in to one of his Western films, *Posse*. Stacy also had another acting success in a TV movie about a veteran amputee called *Just a Little Inconvenience*, but then his life spiraled downward and he ended up being convicted of child molestation and doing time. It was no coincidence that Tarantino chose Stacy and Lancer for the show that Rick Dalton guest stars in.

There was a rumor that one of the long-time movie agents at William Morris, Phil Kellogg, might need a trainee, and I was hoping that was the case, because he really seemed to be an extremely nice man and a true gentleman. His easygoing personality was diametrically opposed to another young hotshot agent there by the name of Mike Ovitz, who had a reputation amongst the trainees to be avoided at all costs because he was a screamer. He screamed at his assistant, he screamed at other employees, he screamed at buyers, the bottom line was that he screamed at everybody except his clients. He was an up and comer at the agency, a pugnacious pit bull of a man and a force to be reckoned with, you just wanted to make sure that you steered clear of him and not get on his bad side. Stan Kamen found out that I was interested in Phil's desk, and he sent an extremely complementary memo to Phil in that regard, so I really started to get my hopes up given how influential Stan was. Little did I know that there was a surprise in store for all of us—it turns out that the Agency was covertly trying to gently coax the beloved Mr. Kellogg into retirement, so there would be no need for a trainee on his desk, which in turn literally left me holding the bag. Because I was perceived by the Agency as so adept at reading scripts and books, and with Stan Kamen's glowing recommendation in my back pocket, there was some talk of assigning me to a literary agent. However, I was still so star struck that I requested to wait for the desk of an agent who represented actors, even if it meant waiting for another opportunity.

Chapter 2

SPAGHETTI MEAL TICKET

That next opportunity arose even quicker than I had hoped, the next most powerful agent in the movie department was Leonard Hirshan, and there was no doubt that his success was completely dependent upon a single client—the strong, squinty eyed and silent cult star of Sergio Leone's "spaghetti" Westerns, the one and only Mr. Clint Eastwood. This reference in *Once Upon a Time in Hollywood* by Tarantino was not as obscure—most fans would know that he was referencing Eastwood when Rick Dalton traveled to Italy to try and revive his career with low budget westerns. Upon his return in the early 1970's, Eastwood had burst into the national consciousness with his portrayal of shoot first and ask questions later, law and order San Francisco cop Dirty Harry. Eastwood's character, who cracked wise and ate hot dogs while casually torturing bad guys, really struck a nerve with the American movie going public, who were weary of the moral morass that the Vietnam war had become. They were starving for a good old-fashioned movie hero who had no such moral ambivalence—Harry knew whom the bad guys were, and he would take care of business, with or without his badge. Eastwood's portrayal would also be helped by the extremely stylish direction of director Don Siegel, a veteran who knew how to crank up the action and tighten the suspense.

"Harry" would become an enormous box office hit and spawn several popular sequels, most of which featured a woman or a black for the conservative Harry to pair up with or play off to the amusement of the audience. Up to this point, his agent Lenny preferred the stability of a secretary rather than the repetitive nature of training young agents in a revolving desk, and his secretary Pam could always be heard in the hallways on the phone sweetly asking "Clint" to hold momentarily for Lenny. Among the trainees, Lenny was known as a brusque, no-nonsense type with a penchant for sarcasm who did not suffer fools gladly, and, like Mr. Ovitz, it was just best to keep your distance rather than risk alienating such a powerful figure in the company. Well, guess who was now headed into that hallowed office to replace his long-time secretary Pam—none other than yours truly! The bravado of my former bouncer status was quickly fading now that I was assigned the intimidating task and hottest of seats of being the middleman between one of the most powerful agents in Hollywood and one of the biggest stars in the world. On top of that, my typing skills were not up to par, as I had been so sure that I was the heir apparent to Mr. Kamen's desk, where my sole duty would have been fielding the dozens of calls that he received daily while leaving the typing chores to his secretary. Well, now I was expected to be Lenny's secretary AND assistant, and I knew that he was mildly annoyed that my skills did not live up to my predecessor. Fortunately, Mr. Kamen once again came to my rescue, as I heard Lenny's side of the conversation as Stan was trying to persuade him that my talents, and future abilities as an agent, more than compensated for my lack of secretarial skills. From that day forward, much to my relief, Lenny was still demanding, but far easier on me than he had a right to be.

Unfortunately, one aspect of the job where I continued to feel awkward was the easy familiarity of show business in general, where everybody called each other by their first names and greeted each other with phony air cheek kisses. I never really felt comfortable addressing Mr. Hirshan as Lenny, although to his credit he insisted on it, but I felt really embarrassed calling Eastwood "Clint." I tried to mimic the informality of former secretary Pam, and I just couldn't pull it off—I sounded phony and disrespectful, although my intentions were to sound like the giddy, enthusiastic fan that I was. I am grateful for the opportunity to recall this embarrassment now, as it has haunted me my whole life. Mr. Eastwood, wherever you are now, I humbly apologize for calling you Clint over the phone!

As I mentioned earlier, there was a cast member from *Shampoo* who would ultimately change my life, and now, working for Lenny, I had the opportunity to come across his work again—former actor turned producer Tony Bill. Not only was Tony the hottest producer in town based on his recent Academy Award winning and huge box office hit movie *The Sting*, which reunited Robert Redford and Paul Newman, the stars of Butch *Cassidy & the Sundance Kid*, but there was an even more interesting buzz amongst the trainees that Tony was different in an extremely important way. He was accessible, which was unheard of in the movies business for such a high profile and powerful producer. One trainee tipped us off that when he had to deliver something to Tony at his newly renovated office building in Venice, a funky beach city near west LA where we had seen Oingo Boingo, Tony not only met him personally, but actually engaged him in some conversation. In other words, Tony was a normal person, not the stereotypical ego maniacal producer who would normally isolate himself even more in the wake of such a huge hit as *The Sting*. We would later learn that Tony's accessibility would encompass the practice of accepting unsolicited screenplays, which turned out to be one of the keys to his success—no producer in town had such a pipeline to successful first-time screenwriters as Tony did.

Tony's mystique piqued my interest for a couple of reasons—one, his appearance as an actor in Warren Beatty's picture *Shampoo* because they had been friendly while both were young actors in the early '60's (Tony replaced comedian Paul Sands, who didn't get along with costar Goldie Hawn). Also, more importantly, because he produced *The Sting* which featured one of my three favorite actors, Robert Redford, and he had acted with my other favorite, Steve McQueen, in *Soldier in the Rain*. To top everything off, Tony was still only in his early thirties, so he was on the verge of a long and lucrative career as a successful producer who could also moonlight as an actor whenever the impulse struck. Lenny's office was currently involved with Tony because Lenny represented a director, Howard Zieff, a successful commercial director who was now directing Tony's new film, *Hearts of the West*, a period comedy about an actor, Jeff Bridges, starring in low budget Westerns. By this time, I must admit that I was having second thoughts about the direction my career was taking at William Morris—as highly as they thought of me, I was still disappointed that I had been unable to train under my mentor, Stan Kamen. Also, as patient as Lenny had been with me, I was still intimidated and stressed out by the prospect of continuing to work for him on a long-term basis. I saw Tony's reputation for accessibility as a potential opportunity to bring to his attention the one marketable skill that I had developed at William Morris, which was script reading. I figured that anyone who was open to receiving unsolicited screenplays must need help reading them, so I hatched a plan to try to segue from the posh offices of William Morris in Beverly Hills to Tony's beachfront offices in funky Venice beach.

Chapter 3

STAR STRUCK

Back at St. Laurence high school in Chicago, I had become increasingly intrigued by the movies due to the actor profiles in *Esquire* and the film reviews of *Chicago Sun Times* film critic Roger Ebert (this was still the time before he created his popular TV show *Sneak Previews* with fellow Chicago critic Gene Siskel for public television). Ebert had an easy-going, personal prose style that invited you to discover the wonders of the movies that he was recommending, and one such movie at that time was *Butch Cassidy and the Sundance Kid*. Although Ebert and another influential critic, Pauline Kael, did not particularly like the film, it sounded so different that I felt compelled to see it.

It is not overstating it to say that seeing that movie on a Sunday night in a suburb of Chicago in 1969 changed my life. It was the summer after I had just graduated from high school, and I was extremely uneasy about my future and what life had in store for me. I was planning on going to college at Southern Illinois University in the hopes of walking on their football team and buying enough time to figure out what my career path would be. I have not had many epiphanies in my life, but seeing that movie was one of them. I was familiar with the movies of Paul Newman at that time, but I had never heard of his costar, Robert Redford, and his performance in that film as the Sundance Kid had an incredible impact on me. It was such a combination of understated cool and sex appeal that I decided that I wanted to transform his performance into my own personality—I would be the Sundance Kid in my own life going forward!

Redford was so impressive in that film that I decided that I wanted to follow in his footsteps and become an actor as well, so at least now I had an idea of what I could study in my upcoming years at SIU—I would be a drama major specializing in acting. Fortunately for Redford, I was not the only one to recognize his star power, and the media quickly crowned him as the fastest rising star in Hollywood after years of him playing second fiddle to his female costars like Natalie Wood and Jane Fonda. Even though he had appeared in the Broadway hit and subsequent film *Barefoot in the Park*, it was widely seen as a hit due to the writing of the author, Neil Simon, more so than the performances, effective as they were.

Not surprisingly and much to my delight, *Esquire* soon offered its own profile of Redford called, "Oh You Sundance Kid" written by journeyman actor but notable literary talent Laurence Luckinbill, and the profile confirmed what I had secretly hoped. Redford was indeed as cool a person as the antihero outlaw whom he had portrayed, with the additional good news that he was a Hollywood outsider who had a normal marriage to a Mormon wife, and they kept their family life far from the maddening Hollywood crowd in the scenic mountains of Utah. The profile and the anecdotes that Redford revealed in it just reinforced my notion that I had chosen the right person as my role model, so I embarked on my college career secure in the knowledge that I could study my craft and forge an acting career in the footsteps of my idol.

Now you can see why the prospect of possibly working for super producer Tony Bill was so appealing to me. Not only was he good enough friends with Beatty to be recruited into his film *Shampoo*, but he had also just re-united the Butch Cassidy trio of Newman, Redford and director George Roy Hill to create one of the most successful movies of all time, *The Sting*. On top of all that, he had a reputation of being friendly and accessible to boot! It was time to venture into Venice, and fortunately, I did not have to travel very far. One of the young agents at William Morris, Robert Stein, had set me up with a small apartment in his building in Venice, so I was already a Venice beach resident and Tony's refurbished art deco building was less than a mile down the street from me. I took a deep breath and walked into Tony's building and luckily, his staff turned out to be as friendly as his reputation. Tony had two assistants, Wendy Riddle and Judy Lange, and they were kind enough to listen to my story of wanting to be a script reader for the hottest producer in Hollywood, even though I only had a year and a half of work experience as a William Morris trainee under my belt. Instead of giving me the polite brush off, they instead introduced me to Tony's story editor, Marian Brayton, who also turned out to be as friendly as the reputation. In a matter of minutes, I was desperately hoping that I could pull off this walk-in attempt and join this staff of incredibly nice people—it seemed like a fantasy that was almost too good to be true!

Marian turned out to be an extremely warm, cheerful, and friendly woman who also possessed the street-smart savvy of a former New Yorker, as she had an extensive background in the book publishing business. One of my speculative theories turned out to be true, as they had been overwhelmed by script submissions because of Tony's reputation, so it turned out that they could use another set of eyes to wade through the dozens of scripts that they were constantly receiving. All a would-be screenwriter had to do was sign a release form, and somebody on Tony's staff would at least start to read their material and Tony would give them a handwritten response. This was all any would be screenwriter could hope for, so hundreds of writers made their pilgrimage to Tony's doorstep to sign said waiver. Apparently, Marian was impressed with my sincere desire to help them scan all the screenplays, so she walked me in to introduce me to Tony himself.

I had gone over in my own mind a hundred times what I would say if given the opportunity to meet Tony. I was determined to let him know what an influence Beatty and Redford had already been in my young life, and how this would be an incredibly motivating factor in working for someone who was so connected with both. I also tried to emphasize all the reading that I had done for Stan Kamen, as I knew that Tony had just dealt with William Morris on the *Hearts of the West*.

Tony listened to all of my reasoning patiently, and I'm sure with a sense of bemusement, at this young guy from Chicago who was so star struck, and told me that he would get back to me in terms of my request to join the staff as a reader. Marian also assured me that it had gone well, and that they would get back to me in due time. As naive as I still was, even I realized that I had better not leave it to chance, so I had both Stan and Lenny from William Morris make calls for me to Tony. It is now incredible to me that these two super heavyweights of the Hollywood agency business took the time to truly help me out, and it speaks volumes for their worth as great people that they did so—I will remain forever grateful to them both. I was about to learn, however, that no matter how much something seemed like a sure thing, sometimes that pitcher called Life throws you a huge curveball.

That next week Marian called me with the bad news—nothing against me, the meeting with Tony had gone well, it was just that a close friend of Tony's, a production manager named Hannah Hempstead, was in between jobs and Tony agreed to hire her as a freelance script reader for the next few months. Although I was devastated, Marian, the kind lady that she was, encouraged me to hang in there and keep in touch.

In retrospect, it was probably just as well that I did not get the job at that time, that probably would have been too much good fortune for me to handle, making me think that life was a piece of cake, that things came too easily. It also taught me the hard lesson that no matter how promising a job situation seems to be, make sure that a job offer is made before leaving the current job. In my mind, I needed to leave William Morris to receive the recommendations from the super agents, but my good intentions not to deceive the agency about my intentions backfired.

Besides, William Morris had its own issues to deal with at the time—it turns out that there had been a palace coup brewing, and five of their top agents, at least one from every department, had decided to break off and form their own agency, Creative Artists Agency. Moreover, which one of the five was now the head of the new agency—none other than Mike Ovitz, the screamer that the trainees had dreaded! The move sent shock waves through Hollywood that would last for years to come, and Ovitz went on to build one of the highest profile and controversial careers in the business. His reputation lives on, as his character was briefly featured in a key scene in *Super Pumped,* the TV movie about the rise and fall of Uber.

Meanwhile, I had assumed that I would be able to return full time to my former moonlighting position as a nightclub bouncer if everything fell through as it had, but even that type of job was not forthcoming, so I was up the proverbial creek without a paddle. I then went through the arduous process of trying to apply for another job that I thought that I might like on a temporary basis, being a golf starter for an LA city municipal course. Even though I did very well on the written test, it became an extremely long, ongoing process. In fact, it took so long that three months had passed, and I received a surprise call from Marian at Tony Bill's office. Tony's friend Hannah had gotten another gig, so they could now bring me aboard as a free-lance script reader, meaning that I would pick up the scripts and books from their office and bring them back to my Venice apartment to "cover" them, and would be paid by the script and book as I returned them. I was ecstatic, I now literally had my foot in the door to my dream job! Humbled by my experience of leaving William Morris without a job in hand (I informed Stan that Tony had hired me, and he wrote me back an incredibly nice and encouraging letter), I was extremely determined to prove to Marian and Tony that they had done the right thing by taking a chance on me. Little did I realize at the time what a glamorous and volatile world I was entering at "Market Street."

Chapter 4

MAVERICK OF VENICE

It did not take long for me to realize that Tony, in the aftermath of the wild success of *The Sting*, had purposely set up shop one block from the funky Venice Beach scene as far away, both physically and spiritually, from the studio system as he could get. Tony got his start in show biz immediately upon graduation from Notre Dame when he was cast as Frank Sinatra's younger brother in the smash hit movie *Come Blow Your Horn*. This was in the early 1960's when the old-fashioned studio system was just starting to undergo a transformation to more independent minded films, but not too late for Sinatra to put Tony under contract with his own film company. During this time Tony carved out quite a career as a secondary leading man to not only Sinatra, but also such huge stars as Rock Hudson in *Ice Station Zebra,* a young Steve McQueen in *Soldier in the Rain,* and Anthony Quinn in *Flap*. But, surprisingly, Tony soon grew weary of the lifestyle of a movie actor, and decided embark on a career behind the cameras in movies.

In retrospect, it is amazing how many unknown filmmakers who later became huge figures in the business Tony befriended during this time, including Francis Ford Coppola (appearing in his first film, *You're a Big Boy Now*), Stephen Spielberg and Terrence Malick. In fact Tony bought and produced Malick's first screenplay, an "existential truck driver movie" featuring Alan Arkin called *Deadhead Miles*. Although the movie was not widely released, Tony realized that this was the niche that he wanted to carve out for himself as a producer—recognizing and giving breaks to first time screenwriters. His next project, *Steelyard Blues,* also featured a script by a first timer, David Ward, which tried to strike a nerve with the anti-war movement by casting such liberal war protesters Donald Sutherland, and, notoriously, Jane Fonda, but the film did not catch on despite the star power of those lead actors.

This is where Tony would make his mark in film history, however—while most producers would shy away from working with the screenwriter again after an unsuccessful film, Tony was receptive to listening to Ward's next idea, a story about two con men teaming up in 1930's Chicago to fleece a gangster, and the rest is history. Tony bankrolled the script and brought it to the powerful producing team of Richard Zanuck and David Brown, and they were able to re-unite the team *of Butch Cassidy*, Redford, Newman, and director George Roy Hill, to the delight of fans worldwide. *The Sting* became one of the most successful films in history, winning every Academy Award it was nominated for except for Best Actor (Jack Lemon beat out Redford with *Save the Tiger*, much to my disappointment), and in the process set box office records worldwide.

Thus, Tony was able to makeover a two-story building on Venice Beach into an art deco style movie production office building called Market Street and escape the studio system that made him a young movie star. Right before Tony set up shop in Venice, he had had some sort of studio deal with MGM, but he was weary of studio politics, and the wild success of *The Sting* enabled him to strike off on his own and bankroll his own development projects. The success of the *The Sting* did not come without a price, however—Tony decided to break off his partnership with Michael and Julia Phillips, his producing partners on *Steelyard Blues* and, along with Zanuck/Brown, on *The Sting*. Although Tony had originally brought them in for their financial expertise, the success of *The Sting* brought out the worst in the egomaniacal, tart tongued Julia Phillips, and Tony did not want to continue his business dealings with the industry with such a temperamental and controversial partner. Thus, they settled their last project together, the controversial Martin Scorsese film *Taxi Driver* as a "Bill/Phillips production", and parted ways. The film itself was a great success, however, featuring an extremely disturbing performance by the young New York actor Robert De Niro, including the memorably haunting "You talking to me?" sequence which would go down in film history as a signature moment for the rising young character star.

At this point any heavyweight industry producer would have given up their parking spot at The Ivy restaurant for the opportunity to hook up with Tony, the hottest producer in Hollywood (as so decreed by, once again, *Esquire* magazine). Much to the surprise of the industry at large, however, but not to those who knew Tony well, Tony instead decided to partner up at MGM with a prestigious New York theatre director, Ulu Grosbard. At that time Ulu had but two feature directing credits under his belt, his own adaptation of his huge Broadway hit *The Subject Was Roses*, and the offbeat *Who is Harry Kellerman and Why is he Saying Those Terrible Things About Me*, featuring Dustin Hoffman.

Hoffman was one of the hottest young stars in Hollywood coming off his performance in *The Graduate*, a film which struck a nerve with an entire generation that was seeking to reject the values of their parents' suburban lifestyle and instead indulge in whatever lifestyle that would make them "happy." The fact that Hoffman was not the stereotypically handsome leading man such as the Rock Hudsons and Robert Wagners of the '60's made him even more endearing to his counterculture audience. I give Hoffman credit, as after *The Graduate*, he had his pick of any hot project in town, but instead chose to pay back his former mentor Grosbard, who had hired him as a stage manager for the off-Broadway production *A View from the Bridge*, featuring then unknown actors Jon Voight and Robert Duvall.

I was proud of myself for knowing all of this about Ulu and guess where I had found all of this out—yep, *Esquire* magazine, which had a lengthy cover story on Hoffman in the aftermath of *The Graduate*. My precocious penchant for reading *Esquire* as a teenager was starting to pay off big time! Tony and Ulu had their own production company at MGM, but Tony grew weary of working under the old studio system and was intent on bringing fresh screenwriting talent to the movies, and thus Market Street was born.

Upon meeting Ulu, I quickly understood why Tony had chosen him to partner up with—he was an incredibly intelligent and creative man, yet had none of the pretensions of being a star director on Broadway, a status that he had deserved with the aforementioned *The Subject was Roses* featuring a then unknown actor named Martin Sheen. Ulu had a very friendly, upbeat, and energetic personality and I could see where Tony found him to be the quintessential person to discuss material with as they both had incredibly high standards when it came to evaluating the literary merits of both screenplays and books. Add savvy Marian to the mix and there was probably not going to be a great literary property or writer around either coast that they did not know about.

I will be forever grateful that Ulu warmly welcomed me into the Market Street mix, as I felt that he sensed my sincere desire to help them seek out quality material for their company to become involved with. Speaking of the theatre, since I at least had some sort of day job, I decided the time was right to try and fulfill another one of my ambitions, which was to take acting lessons from the same teacher that Warren Beatty had studied under, Stella Adler. She came out to LA during the summers, so I enrolled in two of her classes, the fundamentals, and an audit of her scene class. I was thrilled when she gave me a complement during a class, but the most memorable aspect of the class was a striking young would-be actress I met there and befriended named Melanie. She had spent time in New York and was pretentious as all get out, but I had a crush on her even though she was happily married. I befriended her anyway and our most intimate moment occurred when I invited her to come with me on one of Tony's spontaneous sailing outings. Just when I thought I was king of the world, I became seasick over the side of the boat. That was the end of any romantic overtures that I may have had in mind for that day!

As I made my frequent visits to Market Street to pick up and drop off scripts and books, I quickly realized what kind of dynamic Tony was trying to create at Market Street. He either rented out or gave away office space to anyone in the business that needed a temporary respite from the backstabbing grind of the movie business, including screenwriters that needed a haven for their creative juices to flow, so the current tenants comprised an extremely colorful cast of characters. One thing I quickly realized about Tony was what I liked to describe as him being an "equal opportunity socializer." Any other producer in his shoes of success would have indulged in all the vices that money can buy, including booze, drugs and women, but Tony was happiest when he hosted sailing cruises for his friends, or poker parties at Market Street for his inner circle of long time show biz buddies, including his agent, Bill Robinson. He was equal opportunity though because he also hosted poker parties for low rollers like his staff and acquaintances, including me, and he was just as happy to have a beer with us and play for the low stakes that we could afford. In fact, Tony once spontaneously came over to my little Venice apartment to watch a Notre Dame football game with me, and after a few beers I was trying to demonstrate on him what a clipping penalty was! Tony was also impressed that there was a book on my mantle written by his good friend Nicholas Meyer, who wrote the very well received book turned movie, *The Seven Per Cent Solution*.

Another example of Tony's social generosity is that he received screening passes to every movie being released in Hollywood, but he rarely attended himself, even though it would have raised his already high profile even higher—instead, he gave the passes to his staff, including me, and we were able to bask a little bit in the spotlight of Hollywood. One of the only screenings that Tony personally attended was the initial screening of his friend George Lucas' movie, and even then, he took me and his assistant Wendy along with him. The movie was *Star Wars*, and now Wendy and I can look back and say that we were a part of film history by attending the first ever screening of the ground-breaking film.

Tony's reputation was such that people in the industry would even reach out to his staff like myself so that they could feel a little connected.

I once attended a dinner party hosted by Winter Horton, a young relative of the famous movie star Edward Everett Horton, and I really received a taste of old time Hollywood glamour and formality.

I also became adept at spotting even the most minor celebrities in public, and I once approached a young actress in a Marie Cullender's restaurant, of all places, to let her know that I enjoyed her work on a then popular TV series called *James at 15*. The actress was Terri Nunn, and she later became the lead singer of the world-famous glam rock band Berlin.

Even though Tony literally had hundreds if not thousands of acquaintances, including some of the highest profile heavyweights in the film business like Lucas, Coppola, Spielberg, Milius, and Malick, I soon learned that he had a relatively small circle of intimate friends that he liked to keep close at hand by either giving them office space at Market Street or making sure that they were frequent visitors there. These friends included the aforementioned production manager Hannah Hempstead; the aforementioned photographer, film historian and up and coming screenwriter Curtis Hanson, who had contributed photos to the Bonnie and Clyde book and was also good friends with screenwriter Robert Towne; new screenwriter Bob (no relation to Dino) DeLaurentis, who had been recommended to Tony by a friend while Bob was waiting tables back East; and Bruce Paltrow, a fledgling TV writer whose wife, Blythe Danner, had just appeared in Tony's movie *Hearts of the West*. In fact, Tony was such good friends with them that he helped Hannah and Curtis get their own film, *Little Dragons*, off the ground.

Fortunately for me, by now Tony was really impressed with my script coverage, and he was gracious enough to sing my praises to all his friends. They were all particularly amused by the fact that I wrote out all my coverage in long hand since I still had not honed my typing skills. In fact, Tony was so impressed by my ability that he offered me the dream job that I had been hoping for: since Marian was now considered a VP, I could shed my freelance status and move into an office in Market Street as a full-time salaried story editor for Tony and Ulu! I was ecstatic—not only was I now one of the few staff members for one of the most prestigious companies in the movie business, but I would also now be able to interact with all the Market Street tenants and friends of Tony daily. As a bonus, I would also now be able to park my ten-speed bicycle as Tony also allowed me to use one of his cars, a 1968 Mustang convertible—talk about Hollywood perks!

I could not believe how it was all coming together for me—in my own mind, I was now on the inside of the Beatty/Redford/Bill axis! Even more impressively on a day-to-day basis, all the friends and tenants of Market Street warmly accepted me. I was now able to go to lunch on a regular basis with Bruce Paltrow, Curtis Hanson and Bob DeLaurentis to a tiny cafe up the street called Maxwell's, where we would talk endlessly about basketball and movies—it was our own version of the hit movie that was to be made years later called *Diner* starring Mickey Rourke. Other writers and staff members, like Alan Swyer (writer of *The Buddy Holly Story*) and Michael Kane, joined us at various times over the years, but the four of us were the constant core of this lunchtime gab fest for the next four years.

Bruce Paltrow was married to actress Blythe Danner and was one of the funniest and most good-hearted people I have ever met. He kept up a constant stream of stand-up insult humor in the vein of the popular comedian at the time, Don Rickles, and nobody was spared as a target of his pointed comical insults, not even Tony, who laughed as hard at himself as anybody. I also accepted the harmless insults with good nature, but I was able to get off a one liner of my own that Tony got a kick out of when Bruce questioned my ability to get female companionship. Let's just say that I hinted things happened at his home while he was out of town, and, to his credit, he took as good as he gave. Also, to his credit, he had toiled for quite a few years to get a TV pilot off the ground as producer and writer, and it finally happened with, of all people, Ethel Merman. The show did not last long but it was enough to get his foot in the door, and Bruce would go on to create two of the most memorable shows in TV history, which I will detail later.

In the meantime, some more William Morris karma intersected Market Street as Lenny's director client, Howard Zieff, needed a synopsis written on a book project that he was trying to pitch, so since he had directed *Hearts of the West* for Tony, he called Tony and asked him to recommend somebody. Tony was kind enough to recommend me, on the condition that I would need to type this synopsis instead of the handwritten ones I was doing for him and Marian. When Zieff asked Tony how he would know it was me when I came to meet with him, Tony said just look for Lewis Tater, the character that Jeff Bridges played in *Hearts*. This was both a complement, since Bridges was obviously a handsome young man, but also an amusing jab at the naiveté that Tony felt I shared with that character.

Zieff, having come out of the world of TV commercials to become a director, was a throwback in that he was a fast-talking pitchman, but I enjoyed meeting him and successfully wrote the synopsis for his book project. Tony was graciously starting to get me what everyone needs to be successful in the movie business—exposure.

Chapter 5

THE UNKNOWN COMIC

One of Tony's less successful efforts in the aftermath of *The Sting* was a big budget opus called *Harry and Walter Go to New York*. On the surface it seemed to have a lot going for it—a star cast lead by James Caan, coming off the enormously successful gangster saga *The Godfather*. It was directed by Tony's good friend Francis Ford Coppola, for whom Tony had appeared as an actor in Coppola's first film, *The Big Bounce*. I had become a fan of Caan since Stan represented him and I was his script reader at WMA. A side note coincidence—Caan also played ill-fated Chicago Bears running back Brian Piccolo in the classic TV movie *Brian's Song*, and I had met the real Piccolo while I was a teen age caddie back in suburban Chicago. Piccolo's friend and teammate, the Bears Hall of Fame running back Gale Sayers, became the athletic director at my alma mater, SIU, where my brother Bruce had worked for him!

The other headliner was Elliot Gould. everybody's counterculture favorite based on his popular role as one of the rebellious surgeons, along with Donald Sutherland, in the hit film *M*A*S*H*. Michael Caine, the quintessentially classy British actor who had skyrocketed to fame as the womanizing cad in the film that captured the mod style of the swinging '60's London, *Alfie*, rounded out the star-studded cast. The appeal of the project for Tony was that it was being produced by two of his best friends, Don Devlin and Harry Gittes– Devlin had just produced another buddy opus, *The Fortune*, starring Warren Beatty and Gittes's buddy, Jack Nicholson. Both Devlin and Gittes would also produce another Nicholson film, *Going South*, in another couple of years, so it was all one big happy family. In fact, Nicholson and Gittes were such good friends that Nicholson's character in the subsequent film, *Chinatown*, was named after him—J.J. Gittes. Tony was also fond of the script which had been written by a first-time screenwriter, John Bynum. Stan Kamen had made sure that it was a William Morris client "package" by persuading the producers to hire his director client, Mark Rydell, coming off another Caan film, the downbeat but critically well received *Cinderella Liberty*.

Just like when a group of star players does not necessarily make for a winning sports team, this high-powered package of star talent did not click, and the film fizzled at the box office. In Tony's mind, the blame could be solely attributed to the director, whom Tony felt unnecessarily re-wrote what was already a charming script just so he could exert the power of a director's ego.

The saving grace of the film was the classy Caine, and I was about to have my own up close and personal encounter with him. Tony's production associate friend, Hannah, was assembling a crew for a week's worth of location shooting in Las Vegas for Caine's new film, *Silver Bears*. Tony, Hannah, and Curtis Hanson all felt that it would be a great learning experience for me to actually work on the set of a film, so I was hired to be a production assistant. Even though it was a lightweight caper film, it was being directed by a well-regarded Czech director, Ivan Passer, who would later direct the classic neo noir, *Cutter's Way*, featuring none other than Jeff Bridges. In addition to Caine, it co-starred Bridge's *Last Picture Show* actress, Cybil Shepard, who was still riding her *Picture Show* coattails and had yet to transition to her hit TV series *Moonlighting*, which also featured a wise cracking young actor named Bruce Willis.

I was anxious and excited to get my feet wet on the actual shooting of a movie, not to mention the working vacation locale of Las Vegas for a week—what had I done to deserve all these great breaks in the business? Apparently, Tony had spoken so highly of me to his friends Hannah, Curtis, and Bruce Paltrow that they all went out of their way to help me whenever they could. On the first day of shooting, I introduced myself to Caine since I knew that he had just worked with Tony, and in his own charmingly eccentric style he henceforth called me Bill for the rest of the shoot as he had mixed up my first name with Tony's last name during my self-introduction! I was not about to correct him, so I had to be particularly aware when Michael called out for "Bill" when he needed something. It was a small price to pay given that a star of his magnitude was even acknowledging my existence! His co-star, Cybil, acknowledged me in a more playful way later in the shoot—between takes, she was lying on a couch, and she purposely kicked the tail of my jacket up while I was not looking, then gave me a coquettish smile. I contend to this day that that was her way of flirting with me, only I was too oblivious to realize it at the time.

There was one other memorable aspect to that week—the director, Passer, had seen an unknown comedian at a comedy club on the Sunset Strip and was so impressed with him that he decided to cast him in a small supporting role. What had impressed me was that during lunch breaks, instead of dining with the other actors as he had a right to do, the comedian instead chose to have lunch with us, the crew, and we were all amused by his nonstop stream of hilarious banter—his name? Jay Leno.

Chapter 6

━━━━⟨≋≋≋⟩━━━━

CHICAGO HEARTBREAK

If anyone ever lived up to the expression that actions speak louder than words, it was Tony's friend Hannah Hempstead, who not only set me up with the Vegas job, but she also made sure to include me as an extra in another film she was working on called *Bittersweet Love*. It was not a speaking role, but I was included in a reaction shot as a student catching his teacher kissing her boyfriend, so I felt that my stint at Stella Adler's class had finally paid off in my method acting facial expression. Fresh off that exhilarating stint of working on both of those films, however briefly, I was even more bound and determined to find a project for Tony and Ulu to make together, so I dove headfirst into the pile of scripts and books on my desk.

I came across a book in "galley proofs" form, which meant that it had not been published yet, so I was eager to see if I could recommend something where the film rights might still be available. The book remains to this day the most powerful emotional reading experience that I have ever had. The story was about a teenager in Chicago who tries to commit suicide after the accidental death of his brother, and how he ultimately comes to terms with it with the help of a sympathetic psychiatrist and despite the negligence of an emotionally repressed mother. Being as tuned in as I was to the potential for acting in material, I strongly felt that this role of the vulnerable teenager had the potential to rank with the roles that James Dean played in his prime in the late 1950's, *East of Eden* and *Rebel Without a Cause*. Even more relevantly to Tony, however, I felt that the role of the sympathetic father would strongly appeal to

Robert Redford. I knew from the *Esquire/Luckinbill* profile that Redford had experienced something equally devastating in his own life when one of his children passed away from SIDS. Without being specific, I mentioned this connection that Redford might have to the material to Marian, Ulu and Tony, and both Marian and Ulu read the book based on my recommendation. They agreed that it was powerful, but Ulu's only reservation was that perhaps the story was too "small" for a feature and might work better as a TV movie, which were very popular in the late 1970's. I stuck by my guns and emphasized that I felt the emotional impact and potential appeal to Redford and other star actors would elevate it to feature status.

With Tony's consent, Ulu inquired about the availability of the feature film rights to the heavyweight New York literary agent who had submitted it to them, a young dynamo named Marianne Moloney. It so happened that Marianne was also friendly with both Tony and Ulu, and she broke the bad news to them—the film rights had already been optioned to Wildwood Productions, which was the film company of—Robert Redford! However, it was not the appeal of any of the acting roles for him, he intended to make his debut as a director with this project, *Ordinary People*.

I felt vindicated by my take that Redford would be attracted to the material, but also felt tremendously let down that we would not be involved with the project. On the plus side, I felt that from that day forward, Ulu had a newfound respect for my ability to evaluate material, and we could compare notes in a freer flowing exchange, which was exciting for me. Then I was hit by a blast from the past—the grad student who had directed me in *A Loss of Roses* at SIU, Joe Nunley, received a great review from the LA Times for a play he was now directing in LA, and I agreed to set up a meeting for him and the playwright with Ulu. Ulu was impressed with their passion, and who knew that a couple of Saluki Joes would one day be connected to New York Broadway royalty!

As for *Ordinary People*, I still remained very interested in the progress of the project, particularly in the casting of what I termed the "James Dean" role, and was surprised to learn that Redford went with a relatively unknown actor for it—Timothy Hutton. There was a certain serendipity to the casting, however, in that Timothy was the son of Jim Hutton, a light romantic comedy leading man of the early 1960's who was an acting contemporary of both Redford and Tony—in fact, I wouldn't be surprised to learn that Tony and Jim had competed for some of the same roles back then.

In retrospect, it turns out that every young actor in town, including Tom Cruise, Sean Penn and Rob Lowe had campaigned for the part, but the sensitive Hutton snared it. When I read the role of the earthy, wise cracking psychiatrist, I had originally envisioned comedian Albert Brooks in it, but Redford successfully cast the older Judd Hirsch instead. Donald Sutherland, Tony's star from *Steelyard Blues* was cast in the father role that I had envisioned for Redford, and much to the surprise of everybody in the industry, Redford cast America's TV sweetheart, Mary Tyler Moore, in the role of the tightly wound, brittle and repressed mother. The gamble paid off—Moore won one of many Academy Awards that the film was nominated for, and Timothy Hutton went on to a have a very respectable career as a young leading man, including a disturbing role as a traitor in *The Falcon and the Snowman*, although his career did not possess the meteoric arc that Dean's career did.

To this day, *Ordinary People* is the Big One that got away from me in my fishing expedition for material, but I still feel vindicated by having voiced my opinion about the potential Redford affinity for it. Little did I know that within the year I would be connected to another tragic story of brothers in Chicago.

Chapter 7

⸺∞⸺

MCQUEEN FOR A DAY

Despite the setback of *Ordinary People*, psychologically I was still riding high in terms of considering myself the luckiest guy on earth to be a staff member of one of the hippest movie companies in town, as Tony's unique style and approach to the business continued to generate publicity in the local media. This included a feature article in the *LA Times* which mentioned me as one of the staffers that helped him read all the scripts that were submitted to us, which to me helped solidify my status in the movie business at large.

Although socially I still had my own circle of friends including my former trainee pals from William Morris and a couple of college pals that had moved out to LA, I still liked to go out by myself on weekends and hang out in showbiz bars. I wanted to see if my association with the producer of *The Sting* would score me any points with any actresses, but I was still the fairly shy kid from a small town trying to establish my own identity in the big bad city of false hype, Hollywood. One bar that had a romantic appeal for me was a small restaurant/bar off the coast in Malibu called Crazy Horse, and I have to admit that I was not only looking for female companionship, but I was also hoping that a stray movie star would wander in from that exclusive beach enclave.

One night I was striking out on both counts, but a trio of guys approached me and struck up a conversation with me. It turns out that they had recognized me from a screenwriting seminar that Tony had conducted on a regular basis at an independent film school in Hollywood called Sherwood Oaks (more on that fortuitous connection later as well).

It turned out that all three of them were in the movie business as well—Dan Petrie, Jr., the son of a film director and currently an agent's assistant at ICM, one of the three biggest agencies in town; Michael Meltzer, an assistant to Jon Peters, who was Barbara Streisand's hairdresser and was trying to leverage that position into becoming a film producer (previously mentioned as one of the inspirations for Beatty's film *Shampoo*): and Jim Kouf, a fledging screenwriter. We all hit it off and became fast friends, and we were a precursor to the TV show *Entourage* in that another friend of theirs, Jim's screenwriting partner David Greenwalt, was best friends with, guess who, Jeff Bridges. The only difference with us was that even though we all hung out together, Jeff only hung out with David, as they had a common interest in music. Therefore, we were an entourage by "six degrees of separation" only, but that was good enough for me as they were all good guys, and I really enjoyed their company.

I also did get a brief glance into the private world of the enormously famous Ms. Streisand. Michael had to pick up a script from her house, and I tagged along to keep him company.I was amazed to see that the walls of her room were plastered with newspaper articles and reviews of her! She was well known for having an ego to go along with her talent, and I was seeing the proof of that with my own eyes—her boyfriend Peters also had a reputation for being temperamental, so I can only imagine that their relationship behind these closed doors had to be a volatile one.

Meanwhile, back at Market Street, another project had come about that I was getting excited about—Tony was set to meet with a writer, John Binder, so I was asked to read a script of his to vouch for his writing ability. I was excited to see that it was an adaptation of a novel that I was a big fan of, *North Dallas Forty*, written by rebellious former Dallas Cowboys tight end Pete Gent, one of the only pro football players of his era not to hide his fondness for pot smoking. I was still a huge pro football fan, and the Cowboys were one of my favorite teams due to their colorful quarterback and Gent's teammate and friend, Don Meredith.

The novel was a fictionalized account of their friendship and their rebellion against the Cowboys' straight-laced coach, Tom Landry, and its publication caused quite a stir among the conservative NFL personnel and gave an inside glimpse to curious fans. Binder had been hired to adapt it by maverick film director Robert Altman since Binder had worked on one of his previous films as a script consultant, and the free spirited, counterculture director was a good choice to direct the project although he did not wind up doing so.

I was always big on matching a writer's sensibility to an actor's personality hearkening back to my days at William Morris, and I was relieved to see that Binder's sensibility was a good match for Gent's in the adaptation, and I heartily recommended his writing ability to Tony. Tony then hired Binder to write a screenplay based on his own original idea which came to be titled *Nothing in Common*, about a construction worker who falls in love with a Beverly Hills socialite (I suggested the title *Breaking Ground*, but Marian thought that it sounded like a funeral). The main appeal of the script was the macho sensibility that Binder delivered for the character of the construction worker, Duke, and his interplay with the snobbish socialite made for a fun and easy read.

I knew that this character would draw interest from any leading man who knew about it, and I felt that I had to recommend my old "buddy" from my days in the mailroom, Sam Elliott. He had just done a film that many thought would be his breakthrough role, *Lifeguard*, but it proved to be too lightweight in both story and box office to make him a big time star (coincidentally, it was directed by my friend's father, Dan Petrie, Sr.). However, I really believed in Sam's appeal, and I thought that his persona was a perfect match for Binder's charming macho sensibility. I also thought I had the perfect actress in mind to meet his match, a British actress named Leslie Anne Down, who was then starring in the popular BBC TV Masterpiece Theatre mini-series, *Upstairs, Downstairs*. She was the sexiest British actress since Beatty's movie star/ girlfriend Julie Christie (there's that *Shampoo* connection again), and I considered myself to be an expert on the subject.

Tony had recently allowed me to hand deliver a script that our friend Bob DeLaurentis had written to Christie's hotel, and I was lucky enough to behold her natural beauty with my own eyes. There was no doubt that they were both a pair of British bombshells, and I was hoping that Tony would like my idea of using a fresh face for the female lead.

Most importantly, Tony was hoping that this script would be his directorial debut—there was no other project in the hopper that was close to being greenlighted for Market Street. In fact, Ulu had accepted a directing job to take over the reins for his buddy Dustin Hoffman on a crime thriller, *Straight Time*, that Hoffman had gotten cold feet on. Ulu had since gotten "hot" in the business again based on his well-received direction of one of David Mamet's first plays, *American Buffalo*, off Broadway, and I had to admit to Ulu when he asked me to read it that I didn't get it. Ulu patiently explained to me that the key to Mamet's style was the rhythm of the dialogue, and the underlying dramatic subtext that it conveyed.

I was all set to take off for New York to see the play, complements of a plane ticket by Tony, but the trip fell through when my place to stay in New York fell through. I was supposed to stay with my actress friend Melanie, but I think she felt that it would have crossed the lines of our friendship, and she was probably right. Even though I was disappointed, I became excited again when Ulu invited me to visit the set of *Straight Time*, and I was able to score points with an old college friend who was visiting LA, Barb Yench, by taking her with me to the set to get a glimpse of superstar Hoffman.

Although it was not a commercial hit, I continue to feel that *Straight Time* is one of the most underrated crime thrillers of all time, due to the excellent cast which also included Theresa Russell, Gary Busey and Harry Dean Stanton. In fact, Theresa was also good friends with my pals, Mike Meltzer and Jim Kouf, so they invited me to have dinner with them one night, and Theresa was as sultry in person as she was on the screen, possessing a Lauren Bacall-like smoldering sexuality. Yep, I was living the dream.

Back at Market Street, Tony received the wakeup call of a lifetime one morning. Unbeknownst to all of us, Tony had given the script of

Nothing in Common to none other than his old acting buddy from *Soldier in the Rain*, Steve McQueen, and McQueen had called him at home at 6 o'clock in the morning to tell him that he wanted to do it! Make no mistake about it, a call from McQueen was as sure a way to "greenlight" a project as there was in this town. I was ecstatic but not surprised— the story of the construction worker who loved the society girl exactly mirrored McQueen's own volatile relationship with the popular and well-educated actress Ali McGraw, which made national headlines during the Sam Peckinpah directed action thriller, *The Getaway*. I am positive to this day that McQueen felt that our project would be an emotional catharsis for him in the wake of that relationship.

An argument could be made that McQueen was the biggest movie star in the world from 1965 to 1980 and the role that forever etched him in the public consciousness was as the taciturn San Francisco police lieutenant Frank Bullitt in the 1968 hit movie *Bullitt*. McQueen had enlisted a then unknown British director named Peter Yates to turn an ordinary crime thriller novel into one of the most memorable police films in history by adding a car chase scene featuring McQueen in a 1968 Ford Mustang fastback against the mob villains in a Dodge Charger. To this day the harrowing chase through the hilly streets of San Francisco remains one of the greatest chase scenes in film history. McQueen had already established himself as an action hero to be reckoned with in such films as *The Magnificent Seven* and *The Great Escape* (featuring McQueen in a legendary motorcycle chase), but Bullitt elevated his stardom to a whole different level. His stoic portrayal of the antiestablishment police lieutenant redefined the term "cool" for a whole generation of adolescent males, including yours truly. There was also a mysterious aura to his off-screen personality of a bad boy loner who loved racing that made him a sex symbol to the ladies in competition with his main rival of the sixties, Paul Newman, but McQueen's surly personality greatly contrasted Newman's affable, beer drinking everyman persona.

In fact, it was that off screen competition which made their appearance together in the disaster movie *The Towering Inferno* so compelling—McQueen's no nonsense Fire Chief in the film similarly contrasted Newman's performance as the beleaguered architect. Tony and McQueen knew each other while starring together in a comedy drama in the early 1960's called *Soldier in the Rain* (based on a book by William Goldman, writer of *Butch Cassidy*), and they would continue to kid each other over the years about how bad they both were in the film in that it was an early effort in both of their budding careers. They also shared a passion for antique cars and would buy and sell from each other as the occasion arose.

Even though McQueen now had a reputation for being totally inaccessible when it came to considering projects, and in fact charged producers $1 million dollars just to READ their scripts, Tony and McQueen were so friendly that McQueen agreed to read *Nothing in Common* himself for free. It also probably didn't hurt that Tony was now one of the most successful producers in town, and the naturally distrustful McQueen was comfortable enough with Tony to accept him as the director of the project. I was also on cloud nine in that I was confident that I would be involved in the project as some sort of associate, and that would be the ultimate payoff for my association with Tony.

McQueen was such a huge star that any of his films going forward were destined to go down in film history, for better or worse. Once again, Tarantino was aware of McQueen's stature in film lore, thus the scene in *Once Upon a Time in Hollywood* where McQueen tries to explain who was sleeping with who at the Playboy party. I received an incredible surprise even earlier than I had anticipated, however, when Tony brought McQueen into Market Street after they had lunch in Venice and personally introduced me to him! McQueen smiled and shook my hand, and to this day that encounter remains the biggest thrill that I have ever had, and I will remember it for as long as I live.

Now all we had to do was sit back and wait for the deal to be made while excitement would continue to build throughout Market Street. As if that weren't exciting enough, my social life was also starting to pick up in terms of my relationships with two women I had come to know, both actresses whom I had met through Market Street. Meridith Baer was a New York print ad model who came to LA and became a successful exploitation movie actress, but she wanted to write a screenplay based on her teenage years as the daughter of a prison warden. Tony, as he was inclined to do, supported her dream by giving her an office at Market Street to write it. Meridith was extremely attractive, both physically and spiritually, and had an incredibly open and friendly personality—I immediately developed a huge crush on her. I desperately wanted to have a romantic relationship with her, but I was too intimidated by her popularity to risk any type of advance—she was already in the process of dating some of the most eligible bachelors in town, and I felt that she was totally out of my league. She did respect my position with Tony, however, and we became close friends and confidantes, especially since we saw each other in the office almost every day.

I had a little bit better luck with another well-known actress named Joanna Cassidy, and she made one of the most memorable entrances to Market Street of all time—she roller skated right in, right down the hall, and right into my office looking for Tony. Even though I was flabbergasted to encounter this sexy red head in shorts on roller skates, I had the presence of mind to give her my card. Shortly thereafter, she appeared as a femme fatale in a major film, *The Late Show*, and that fed right into my ultimate fantasy. I had become a big fan of the film noir genre thanks to Ulu's producer friend Jerry Bick, who also had an office at Market Street and was trying to get a re-make of the classic film *Out of the Past* off the ground.

Little did I ever dream that I would become involved with an actress playing a femme fatale, but I also hoped that I wouldn't end up as the fall guy as the male characters usually did in film noir. Here was the real kicker—her best friend was none other than British bombshell Fiona Lewis, whom I mentioned in chapter one as one of the nude models in the scandalous magazine *Oui* that I had managed to buy as a teenager! Furthermore, Fiona had once dated my friend and lunch partner at

Market Street, writer Curtis Hanson! Fiona had since graduated to being a legitimate feature film actress, though her best known role required her to swing naked on a chandelier in a film directed by bad boy British film maker Ken Russell, Lisztomania. You talk about a small world—I had gone from watching Butch Cassidy in a small suburb of Chicago to dating the best friend of the nude model from *Oui*! To me, that was proof that there truly was a God up there manipulating the Universe, and I was living life in the Los Angeles fast lane, whether I liked it or not (I liked it).

We had a couple of dates but my relationship with Joanna did not even develop into a fling, but it was fun hanging out with her and Fiona while it lasted, especially one particular party that they invited me to. At this point in the late 1970's, Venice Beach, which was right outside our door at Market Street, was the most colorful beach scene in all of Los Angeles and was known as Muscle Beach since it was such a haven for bodybuilders—the boardwalk on Venice Beach was like a nonstop twenty-four-hour carnival. Joanna lived in the neighboring beach city of Santa Monica, and she introduced me to her landlord, who turned out to be... Arnold Schwarzenegger! He was the star of that beach scene due to the documentary film featuring him called *Pumping Iron*, but little did I know that I was shaking hands with a future action movie star and governor of California! He did show an early instinct for business, however, by owning those apartment buildings. Whenever I have the chance to recall this brief fling with Joanna, I refer to her most famous role as the "snake lady" from the film *Blade Runner*, and I am not surprised that I did not have a long-term relationship with somebody who was so intimate with snakes!

I did not forget my other actress acquaintance, Theresa Russell, either—I felt that she was right for the lead in another love story that we had in development about a sailor in Long Beach, and I arranged for us to have lunch with Tony down the street from Market Street. Tony knew that Ulu had liked her in his film *Straight Time*, and he agreed that Theresa was right for our script, but the timing was just not right—*Nothing in Common* was on the front burner and it was all hands-on deck.

As I was beginning to realize, sometimes your cup runneth over in the movie biz, and I read another script that I immediately fell in love with, *My Bodyguard* by Alan Ormsby. I mentioned earlier that my new friends, Michael, Jim and Daniel, initially recognized me from when I was a guest panelist at Tony's screenwriting class at Sherwood Oaks Film School. Another teacher from the school, Robert Mundy, recommended a few of the best scripts that had been written by his students to Tony, and Ormsby's script was one of them. The originality of the writing just jumped off the page, and the story was also powerful and heartfelt. One tormentor bullies a new kid at a junior high school, so the kid enlists the help of the scariest kid at the school to take his side and be his bodyguard. The scary kid has a deep and painful secret of his own, and he bonds with his newfound friend. The secret involves the accidental shooting death of his own brother, a story thread amazingly, but coincidentally, like the backdrop of *Ordinary People*.

Once again, I strongly urged Marian, Tony's VP, to read it as soon as possible, and she agreed that we had an uncut diamond of a script on our hands. Although Tony was heavily involved with trying to make the McQueen deal with Warner Brothers, we ganged up on him and insisted that he drop everything and read the whole script, not his usual ten pages glance and then "let's go sailing" cursory read. Tony read it and got excited, as we knew he would, as it was his favorite kind of project- a truly original screenplay by a first-time screenwriter. Tony loved it so much that he decided that he wanted to direct this one as well, and we could line it up in the pipeline to follow *Nothing in Common* with McQueen.

My dreams were coming so true that I was having a hard time realizing when I was awake and when I was dreaming—was I really on my way to becoming a production executive for one of the most prestigious companies in the movie business? It seemed so, because Tony had hired somebody to help us read scripts, a vivacious young woman named Sharon Edict, which meant I was no longer the low man on the short totem pole at Market Street. It was working out perfectly, as Sharon and I hit it off, so I felt that I could mentor her as Marian had done for me.

Meanwhile, Tony did a smart thing—since it was unclear at that point which of the two projects would be "greenlighted" first, Tony accepted an offer from the Learning Corporation of America to direct a short film first, an adaptation of the classic short story, *The Ransom of Red Chief.* This enabled him to get his feet wet as a director before tackling the challenges of a star driven vehicle with McQueen or the equally daunting prospect of directing a cast of junior high school age children. *Red Chief* went without a hitch, highlighted by an amusing performance by Harry Dean Stanton, one of Ulu's actors from *Straight Time*, as one of the beleaguered kidnappers, and I was fortunate to have befriended the film's editor, a smart, sassy young woman named Corky Busman.

The table now seemed to be set for Tony to make his directorial debut on a major Hollywood project, but I should have known that nothing in Hollywood happens that easily. A meeting had been set at Warner Brothers to make sure that everybody was on the same page on *Nothing in Common*, and the meeting was to include Phil Feldman, the president of First Artists, a company that had been formed by a group of stars including McQueen, Paul Newman, Barbara Streisand and Dustin Hoffman as a way for them to stretch their artistic muscles (*Straight Time* had been a First Artists Production); Frank Wells, the Chairman of Warners; John Calley, the Vice Chairman and head of production for Warner Brothers and a longtime friend of Tony; Bill Maher, McQueen's business manager; Phil Parslow from First Artists and Tony himself. The meeting had been intended as just a formality to have all the principals in the same room for the purpose of rubber stamping the elements of the project to greenlight it, but Feldman surprised everyone by flatly stating that First Artists had no intention of becoming involved with the project!

When McQueen, who had a short fuse anyway, found out, he immediately demanded a meeting with Feldman, and then went berserk when Feldman kept him waiting for no reason. McQueen biographer Marsall Terrill chronicled this meeting in his book, *Steve McQueen*, but one detail, his capsule summary of the story line of *Nothing in Common*, was incorrect. To this day, I have been unable to unearth what Feldman's strategy was in throwing this gigantic monkey wrench into such a promising project, but the man had chutzpah, and, contractually, he had the power to veto any First Artists project even though McQueen still owed them one. I will be forever convinced that McQueen was passionate to do it for the catharsis and for the opportunity to work with his longtime friend Tony—I had seen the excitement in his famous baby blue eyes on the day that I had met him.

Chapter 8

⸺⸗∞∞∞⸗⸺

REALITY CHECK

Needless to say, everybody at Market Street, particularly me, was devastated that *Nothing in Common* had gone off the rails, and for such an unusual reason—usually the problem is getting a huge star to commit to your project, not the star's partner arbitrarily vetoing it for no apparent reason. My heart was set on somehow being involved with this project, featuring my boyhood idol, the King of Cool, Mr. Bullitt himself, the one and only Steve McQueen.

As disappointed as I was, however, the timing of the incident benefited my position at the company. Marian had been offered an executive position by her friend at CBS, Donald March, to oversee the development of their movies of the week. Now that *Nothing in Common* had been shelved, at least temporarily, she accepted it, which meant that I was in line to replace her as Tony's VP at Market Street. I honestly did have mixed feelings in that Marian and I were so close professionally, and I truly would miss her cheerful and positive presence around the office. Although I did not expect this to happen so fast for me, I was genuinely excited that I was now second in command, and the only consolation for *Nothing in Common* falling through was that the road was now clear for *My Bodyguard*, which really was my discovery, to now be fast tracked for Tony to make his directorial debut. In fact, Ulu confided in me while I was giving him a ride somewhere that *My Bodyguard* was actually a better project for Tony to start with in terms of there being less pressure than directing the notoriously temperamental McQueen. Although it was hard for me to concede that at the time, in retrospect Ulu was right, as we were all about to find out.

Typical of Tony's nonchalant personality, he did not make a big deal about my promotion, no announcements in the trade papers or anything, but he knew that I would be a loyal and hardworking executive for him. All of my friends at Market Street, Bruce Paltrow, Curtis Hanson, Bob De Laurentis, Jerry Bick and Sharon Edict, were all happy for me, and they all played a huge role in educating me to get to that position. By this time Tony was also giving another newcomer a break, as he hired a recent Notre Dame grad named Mike Roth to be an intern, and I struck up a relationship with him to try and mentor him like Bruce had mentored me. Sharon was promoted into my previous position of story editor, and we even had a little side project that we were working on. A writer whose work I liked, Craig Bolotin, recommended that I read an article/love story in the other Los Angeles newspaper, the *Herald Examiner*, written by a young up and coming journalist. The day that we were supposed to meet with him, however, Tony and I were meeting with Alan Ormsby, the writer of *My Bodyguard*, so Sharon took the meeting with the journalist. His name? None other than Ben Stein, who went on to carve a niche for himself playing supporting comedic roles with his uniquely phlegmatic personality, most notably in *Ferris Bueller's Day Off*. Tony did eventually meet with him and was captivated that he was a former Wall Street expert who decided to pursue the writing muse.

Now things were heating up on *My Bodyguard*. Tony was able to consummate a deal with Mel Simon, a supermarket mogul who had formed his own production company, and Tony brought in one of his best friends, Don Devlin, one of the producers of the ill-fated *Harry and Walter Go to New York,* to produce the film for him. As he had in the past when he hired David Ward to write *The Sting* even after their previous collaboration was not successful, Tony did not let the stigma of Harry deter him from hiring Devlin to be the point man for the most personal film of his career. Tony was the exception in the movie business in terms of his loyalty to his friends and colleagues. He was in it for the long haul, not just for short-term success, and I wish that some of the big names in the film business whom Tony had given their first breaks to had reciprocated in kind, but that was not the nature of the business.

The first thing that Devlin did upon being hired was change the age of the characters in the script. Ormsby had originally written them as being in junior high, and to me that made the bully aspect even more intense and the friendships among the kids even more charming, but Devlin changed them to high school age. At least he let Ormsby write in the change instead of bringing in another writer, as Tony was not a believer in the standard industry practice of bringing in a parade of writers to continually rewrite the script. Then I was included in the first big meeting since being promoted to VP—Tony, Devlin and I met with Devlin's casting director, Vic Ramos, and he was showing us pictures of young actors for the main roles. Up until then, it had been assumed that the key role of the bully should be played by a fearsome looking kid, but when I saw a picture of a good-looking kid, I said stop, that's him- that's the right actor for the role of Moody the bully. Even though he was good looking, he also projected a look that showed that he could also have a mean streak, and I thought that would put a neat twist on the role—one of the popular kids in the school was also the bully! The young actor had only done one other role in a feature film up to that point, a film called *Little Darlings*, and the actor's name was Matt Dillon. Dillon was eventually cast as Moody, and I thought that I had made a solid contribution in my first at bat as a production associate.

Even though things were progressing smoothly on My Bodyguard, John Calley and Warner Brothers had not given up on *Nothing in Common* despite the McQueen falling out, and they suggested Stan Kamen's client and the actor I had recommended for one of his roles, popular country/ rock singer Kris Kristofferson. I had recommended the offbeat script *The Sailor who Fell from Grace with the Sea* for Kristofferson while I was reading for Stan, so I was familiar with his work. But I favored another William Morris client even more, none other than my original idea for the role before McQueen, the only actor who acknowledged my existence while

I was in the mail room, Sam Elliott. I convinced Tony to take a meeting with him, and the three of us squeezed into my Mach 1 Mustang and went to lunch at a local Venice restaurant. I don't remember if there were many females in the restaurant that day, but if there were, they must have been fantasizing a little bit at the sight of both Sam and also Tony, who continued to be movie star handsome in his own right. I must admit that I got a kick out of being able to return Sam's original kindness toward me by setting this up. To his credit, he spent most of the lunch trying to persuade Tony that his current girlfriend, actress Katherine Ross from *Butch Cassidy* (there's that fate again), was right for the role of the socialite in *Common*. The lunch went well, and it was just plain fun to hear a couple of actors who had paid their dues just shooting the breeze about the business. But then it was back to the task at hand, moving *My Bodyguard* slowly but surely toward its production date.

I had always assumed since *My Bodyguard* was my discovery, so therefore, my baby, that I would be involved with it, as I was in the casting meeting, and receive a major "above the line" credit on the film. This was particularly important to me since I cared more about film credit than money at that point in my career, especially in that I was so proud to be associated with Tony. I was making the average amount of salary for a "development" person at a film company at that point, but I was aware that Tony was supporting a full staff at Market Street. Sometimes he had an overhead deal with a studio and sometimes he paid us out of his own pocket, so I honestly had no quarrel with what I was making. Besides, Tony was incredibly generous, I was driving a car that he had paid for, our mutual friend Curtis Hanson had set me up in one of his family-owned apartments in upscale Marina del Rey at far below market value, and the bottom line was that being Tony's VP was my dream job regardless of the salary.

I had determined, given my position with Market Street, that the appropriate title for me on *My Bodyguard* *would* be "associate producer," since I realized that I was not ready for the title of producer yet (I was still only in my late '20's at that point). I was hoping that the fact that it was an above the line credit would reflect my contributions to the project and my close relationship to the director, Tony. If there was room in the budget for a little additional money for me with that title, I wouldn't turn it down, but it was not a deal breaker as far as I was concerned—I just wanted the world to know that I was Tony's right-hand guy.

Earlier in the year, Tony's assistant Wendy had asked me if I wanted a credit on another film Tony had produced in conjunction with his deal with Warner Brothers, *Boulevard Nights*, but I had gratefully declined. I really did not have any input or ties to that project, and I did not want to just gratuitously ride Tony's coattails on it, but I was chomping at the bit to be involved with *Nothing in Common* or *My Bodyguard*. Well, you know what they say about assuming, but in this case, it only made it out of me—Devlin, the producer, decided that he was going to award that credit to his production manager and not include me! Sometimes the production managers get that credit and sometimes they don't, but in this case, Devlin wanted to make sure that he accepted the job, so he gave it to him. I honestly don't remember how or if the news was broken to me, and I know that Tony did not tell me directly, but I knew that I was not getting that credit and I was devastated beyond words. In retrospect, I was still incredibly young and inexperienced, but I just could not figure out how to save face on that one.

Tony did try to make it up to me by setting a meeting for me with the production president of Warner Brothers, Bob Shapiro, because I had another script that I was in love with called *No Small Affair* by Craig Bolotin, the writer who had told me about the Ben Stein article. Coincidentally, Bob and I knew each other because he was a major film agent at William Morris while I was there, so I was not as nervous as I normally would have been in meeting the president of Warner Brothers. There is no getting around it, I choked at that meeting—I forgot the name of the script that I was there to tell him about, and the only saving grace was that Bob was such a gentleman about it rather than throwing me out of his office. I did manage to tell him about the script, but my embarrassment got the better of me. I am sure that Tony and Bob had a good laugh about it the day after, and Tony was also gracious and tried to smooth it over by telling me that he was impressed that Bob had told him that he remembered me from William Morris. There was no consoling me, however, there was no doubt in my mind that I had completely dropped the ball on the biggest meeting of my life. I was somewhat vindicated in that the script eventually was made into a well-received film, but it should have been produced by me if I had done a better job of selling it.

I should have been ecstatic that Tony had tried to set me up with a deal of my own, and should have swallowed my pride that I did not receive the associate producer credit due to the general overall politics of the movie business. I knew that Tony was not unhappy with my work, he would tell anybody who would listen that I was the best script analyst that he had ever seen. He even stated to his class at Sherwood Oaks that he hoped that both Marian and I would work for him forever, and I wanted to, but I just couldn't let it go.

Marianne Moloney, the literary agent who submitted *Ordinary People* to us, was now an executive at Universal, and she was kind enough to take me out to lunch and try to talk me out of it, but I was just too young and immature to see the forest from the trees. I mournfully requested that Tony step into my office (which was a great office, by the way, where I had hung a poster of *The Sting* and my autographed photo of Julie Christie) and told him that I would hold down the fort while he was off shooting in Chicago (a location which I had recommended). However, when the shoot was done, I would resign from my position at Market Street due to my disappointment at not receiving the associate producer credit. I'm sure that Tony realized that I was making a huge mistake (had I not learned from William Morris not to leave a job before I had another one lined up?), but I think he also realized how traumatic the situation was for me. He was considerate enough to allow me to leave with my dignity intact, so he accepted the news stoically.

To add insult to injury, *Ordinary People*, with Redford directing, would also be shooting in Chicago while *My Bodyguard* was there. Therefore, instead of returning to my old stomping grounds as the conquering hero, I would be left behind to count the days until I would vacate my dream job without a clue in terms of what I was going to do next. Believe it or not, my exit would have a positive effect on the personal lives of both Tony and I in the coming years, to be detailed later in the story, but at that time I was as low as I would ever be in my life.

During the five years while I was there, however, I always stated that everybody in the movie business, literally from A to Z, came down to visit or meet with Tony to catch a glimpse of the unique, creative beach office dynamic that he had set up for himself, his staff and tenants. It was the thrill of a lifetime just to see them pass through our doors, and here are the ones that I most remember passing through, from A-Z:

Anne Archer—became a star actress based on her sympathetic performance as the beautiful wife in the hit movie *Fatal Attraction*, came down to pitch a project to Tony.

Lindsay Anderson—the British film director best known for his films starring Malcolm McDowell, *If* and *O Lucky Man*, paid Tony a social visit, and I remember him correcting me when I mentioned England—he said it is not England, it is Great Britain. I was embarrassed as I considered myself an expert on all things British, including films, books music and TV, so I had to eat some humble meat pie in that encounter.

Martin Brest—directed his first movie, *Going In Style*, with Tony producing for Warner Brothers. He hit it off with my colleague, Sharon Edict (later Bernhardt), but he possessed a little bit too much of an egotistical edge in his personality for my taste, so I steered clear of him. So much for my instinct, he went on to direct the Academy Award winning *Scent of a Woman* starring Al Pacino.

Jeff Bridges—Tony's friend and star of Tony's film Hearts of the West and best friends with my friend David Greenwalt, also came down to have lunch with Tony about *Nothing in Common* after McQueen fell through.

Sean Connery—the one and only James Bond, came down to Market Street with Tony's friend, studio executive Mike Medavoy, but everybody at Market Street had gone sailing with Tony except me (I had stayed behind based on my previous experience of "lunch overboard" while sailing with Tony). Therefore, I was the only person left in the building to greet them, so, in this instance, fate was on my side, and take my word for it, Mr. Connery was as charismatic in person as he was on the big screen—I was shaken AND stirred after shaking hands with him!

Steve Dejarnett—another young directing talent that Warner Bros. sent Tony's way to try and shepherd—we did not produce it, but his film, *Miracle Mile*, was eventually made years later starring Anthony Edwards, and Sharon Edict Bernhardt received a thank you credit on it.

Robert Duvall—Ulu's good friend came down to visit Ulu in preparation to star in Ulu's movie *True Confessions*—I will never forget how warmly and effusively they greeted each other, like only lifelong friends can. Not many actors have a better resume of memorable performances than Mr. Duvall—Tony gave me his screening pass to see the first ever screening of *Apocalypse Now*, directed by Tony's good friend Francis Ford Coppola, and it reunited Duvall and Coppola from their huge hit together, *The Godfather*. I took my friend Meridith Baer to the screening, and we were blown away by Duvall's searing performance. I was ecstatic that Ulu had gotten the shot to direct *True Confessions*, as it was a major project based on the critically well received book by John Gregory Dunne, and it was a reward by the powers that be that recognized Ulu's great work on *Straight Time*. I gave Ulu an unsolicited casting suggestion on the actor to play Duvall's brother in the film, a corrupt priest—Sam Shepard, the award-winning playwright who so memorably played pilot Chuck Yeager in *The Right Stuff*, and Ulu was somewhat intrigued with the idea of involving a fellow theatre heavyweight. However, I couldn't quarrel with the choice who was eventually cast—Robert De Niro. The film was not a commercial hit, but I still contend that the acting in it was as good as it gets.

John Frankenheimer—the legendary director of *The Manchurian Candidate* and a contemporary of Ulu, did postproduction on one of his films at Market Street.

Amy Heckerling—yet another young director that Warner Bros. wanted Tony to develop and mentor. We initially had lunch with her and a Warner Brothers executive, and she worked out of Market Street while writing a screenplay. She went on to write and direct the comedy *Fast Times at Ridgemont High*, which was a teen hit and made a star of young Sean Penn. One of the first female directors to have a substantial Hollywood career, she also went on to write and direct the hit film *Clueless*.

Michael Kane—he was one of Tony's favorite success stories—he operated his own soda truck business while writing screenplays on the side, and Tony read one of them and loved it so much that he put Michael under a personal writing contract. Michael was an extremely colorful character, as he had lived some aspects of his life on the edge, and we collaborated on a script together called *Tender War*, a story about how a gambling addiction destroys the relationship between a guy and a vivacious French girl. I had become enamored of the young French actress Isabelle Adjani when Bob DeLaurentis and I visited the set of a movie called *The Driver* and I had seen her striking beauty in person, so I was determined that she would play this role if the script ever got off the ground. It didn't, but I was still proud of the script that Michael had written, it was a powerful, heartbreaking tearjerker. Market Street did not produce any of Michael's projects, but he had a long and successful career as a screenwriter, including *Southern Comfort*, a film by the prestigious director of *The Driver*, Walter Hill, *All the Right Moves* starring Tom Cruise and the Burt Reynolds sequel *Smokey and the Bandit II*. Another side note on *The*

Driver, the production manager on the film whom Bob and I met on the set was named Frank Marshall, and he went on to become one of the most successful producers in film history as Steven Spielberg's producer. I had one more encounter with Frank many years later, as we will see a little later in this story.

John Landis—one of the most influential directors of the '70's in making slob comedies a legitimate genre of film, he used Market Street as his production office for his first low budget comedy, *Kentucky Fried Movie*. In fact, he shot one of the scenes there, where actor Donald Sutherland falls into a cake, and most of the staff at Market Street served as background extras in the scene, including me. Although his high energy personality is reflected in his comedies, I never had the opportunity to get to know him too well, as he was somewhat aloof, but I did get to know his producer, a more jovial sort named Robert K. Weiss. I also became friendly with their production manager Alice West, a cheerful pro who went on to great success in both films and TV. *Kentucky Fried Movie* went on to become a comedy cult hit, and shortly thereafter, Landis went on to direct one of the biggest hits in slob comedy history, *Animal House,* featuring a landmark performance by Saturday Night Live stalwart, John Belushi. Little did I know at the time that I would have the opportunity to befriend another breakout star in this film a little bit later in my career. Producer Weiss went on to also collaborate with Belushi in another hit film, Blues Brothers. Unfortunately, a Landis directed segment in the movie of *The Twilight Zone* was marred by the tragic death of actor Vic Morrow during the shooting of a helicopter scene, and the eventual tragic death of Belushi has also been well chronicled.

Laurence Luckinbill—the aforementioned actor and writer who wrote the *Esquire* profile of Robert Redford that was such an influence on me, also rented an office at Market Street. I regret to this day that I never pulled him aside to tell him that in person. As mentioned earlier, I am essentially a shy person at heart, but I wish I could have put that aside in this case and approached him about how influential his article had been on me.

Malcolm McDowell—The cult star of the Lindsay Anderson films, he also made film history as the malevolent "droog" in the Stanley Kubrick masterpiece, *A Clockwork Orange*—he also paid Tony a social visit, but I did not meet him personally. I was thrilled to see him in person, however, as my college buddy, Fred Hecker, and I still call each other droogs to this day based on our seeing the film together in college. McDowell is still going strong, performing memorably on the hit TV show *Entourage*.

Michelle Phillips—the sexiest member of the popular pop singing group from the '70's, the Mamas and Papas (California Dreaming), Michelle was able to parlay that fame into a career as an actress in films but gained even greater notoriety by becoming the lover of both of our equally notorious friends, Mr. Warren Beatty and Jack Nicholson! Michelle wound up needing an office at Market Street to perform postproduction for a project, and I can't tell you how much I looked forward to going into the office while she was there, California Dreaming big time! She was a great lady—friendly, down to earth, and a little flirty—once again I had a difficult time separating fantasy from reality, my life at Market Street was such a dream come true, but at least I was aware at the time of how good I had it! Once again Tarantino recognized her status on the pop culture scene of the '60's by including her in the party scene at the Playboy Mansion in *Once Upon a Time in Hollywood*. To show you how influential Ulu also was at that time, Tarantino consulted him on his first ever film, *Reservoir Dogs*, and included Ulu in the thank you credits. Tony knew talent when he saw it when he partnered up with Ulu after *The Sting*.

David Putnam—as mentioned earlier, I really was a connoisseur of British films, and I was a big fan of a pair of British rock music movies called *That'll Be the Day* and *Stardust* featuring the real-life British rock singer David Essex. They were a thinly veiled fictional account of the rise and fall of a rock star based on many British musicians of that era, including Paul McCartney. In fact, one of McCartney's contemporaries, lead guitarist Dave Edmunds (I Hear You Knocking), played one of the band members in *Stardust* and I became such a fan of his that I attended every one of his appearances in clubs throughout the '80's, usually dragging my friend Fred along with me. I also attended Essex's real-life concert appearance and enjoyed the Beatles throwback sound of the pop music. I noted that the producer of both films was a dashing young Brit named David Putnam, and I made a mental note to follow his career as a producer. Well, guess who came to Market Street to screen a rough cut of his new film to an invited audience—none other than the outspoken Mr. Putnam. That new film, *Midnight Express*, written by Oliver Stone, became one of the most controversial films of the decade, and, like *Apocalypse Now*, I knew that I was seeing something special and powerful. Once again, Market Street was the happening place to launch film events.

Ron Shelton—Ron was a former minor league baseball player who had written a script based on his experiences, and, like many a first-time screenwriter, he submitted the script to our office. At the time we had a sharp reader named Marie Soule and she passed it along to me to read. It was titled *A Player to Be Named Later* and centered on the relationship between a veteran catcher and a flaky rookie pitcher. I thought it was extremely funny and charming, and even though baseball scripts were thought to be death at the box office, I still agreed to meet with him as his writing style was right up my alley, an ironic combination of macho charm and comic whimsy. He later added a female character, a groupie whom the two players compete for, and the rest is history—the retitled *Bull Durham* became one of the best baseball comedies of all time. It also confirmed the star status of the actor who played the catcher, Kevin Costner (much to the chagrin of Shelton's actor friend Kurt Russell, who thought that he had the inside track for the role). However, Mike Medavoy, Tony's friend and the studio head of Orion who greenlighted the project, insisted on Costner whom he had used in the Navy thriller *No Way Out*. Tim Robbins as the pitcher and Susan Sarandon as the groupie rounded out the wonderfully off beat cast, and the good-natured humor struck a nerve with a widespread audience. Ron and I hit it off personally, and our paths would continue to cross several times later in this story.

Orson Welles—When Orson Welles, the producer, writer, and director of one of the greatest films in history, *Citizen Kane*, walked down the hallways of Market Street on his way to see Tony, I thought to myself, you have got to be kidding me—who is going to walk through our doors next, Marlon Brando? Mr. Welles wanted to revisit the Venice locations that were used in his classic film *The Third Man*, and it really was a tribute to Tony that such an icon came down to meet him in person. I honestly cannot think of any other person in the history of show business who was as connected to the greats of the business as Tony was. Tony is too modest to acknowledge it, but he really was the godfather of new talent in the movie business for the decade of the '70's, and if Kevin Bacon was the king of six degrees of separation, Tony was the man of 1 degree of separation—he either knew or had met every important film talent in the business. It was simply amazing to me that he was able to maintain such an even keeled personality when anybody else in his position would have become an insufferable egomaniac.

Bob Wunsch—Bob had been one of the most high-powered literary agents in the business, but like many before him, decided to don another hat and become a producer. He set up shop in an office at Market Street, and I was a big fan of his first film as a producer, the hit hockey comedy *Slap Shot*, starring Paul Newman, and reuniting him with his *Butch* and *Sting* director, George Roy Hill. Although it was best known for its slapstick take on minor league hockey featuring the antics of the three goons called the Hanson brothers, it really had an originally profane script written by, ironically, a female named Nancy Dowd. Paul Newman as the beleaguered player coach delivered most of these lines, and some of his dialogue is quite disturbing given the lighthearted context of the milieu. It is a credit to both Bob and Hill that they recognized the originality of the dialogue amidst all the slapstick humor.

Michael Ontkean also gave a star making performance as the star player who does not buy into Newman's macho malarkey, but his career took a nosedive shortly thereafter when he played a gay character in the Paul Mazursky film *Willie and Phil*. At that time, the movie going public was still not sophisticated enough to accept gay characters as the leads in a film in the '70's. Fortunately, David Lynch of *Twin Peaks*, would revive Ontkean's career many years later in the cult hit TV show and Tony also wound up directing him in a Christmas time TV movie. Bob Wunsch and I hit it off well because we were on the same wavelength when it came to the value of literary properties, and it also helped that we had the mutual Market Street friend of the irrepressible Mr. Bruce Paltrow.

Zucker Brothers—along with their friend Jim Abrahms, they comprised the writing team for the film *Kentucky Fried Movie* directed by John Landis. Their personalities were truly as zany as the style of their movies, and the way they took over the building of Market Street with their high energy antics really did remind me of the Marx brothers. After KFM they split with Landis and forged a comic style all their own, best displayed in the silly spoof *Airplane*. *Airplane* also made a star out of Leslie Nielsen, an older character actor who struck comic gold with his deadpan performance and went on to star in many other silly Zucker spoofs, including *The Naked Gun* series. Market Street was never so lively as when the Zucker Brothers were roaming the hallways.

In retrospect, I was incredibly fortunate to have been a fly on the wall while all of this tremendous talent passed through Market Street, and I can't imagine that there will ever be another combination of high-powered producer and uniquely restored historic building to draw such a mixed bag of artistic personalities. Market Street literally did transform the sleepy, seedy beach community of Venice into a thriving artistic hub of creativity, and Tony was the Jay Gatsby like host of one very long artistic party there.

Chapter 9

‒‒‒‒‒ ⟨⟨⟨⟩⟩⟩ ‒‒‒‒‒

STONE'S THROW

Even after I vowed to myself after William Morris that I would never voluntarily leave a job again without having another one in hand, here I was, back on the street again, with no immediate prospects in sight. At least this time, however, I had five good years of Market Street under my belt, including the network of good friends that I had made there like Bruce Paltrow and Meridith Baer. By this time Bruce had created a landmark TV show, *The White Shadow*, about a white former pro basketball player who accepts a job coaching at an inner-city high school and it was one of the original "dramedies" on network TV. It became a cult hit, and established Bruce, after years of dues paying, as a bona fide TV producer-writer talent to be reckoned with. I was even able to treat my brother Bruce, who is my best friend, to an on-set visit of the gym while the basketball action was being shot, and I took great comfort in knowing that Paltrow was there for me as a mentor and confidant.

Another writer from Market Street whom I had worked with, Michael Kane, also went to bat for me and recommended me to a true Hollywood heavyweight producer, Lawrence Gordon, and I really enjoyed meeting him. He was a tough talking, old school kind of producer, and he was looking for somebody to replace his associate, Frank Marshall, whom I had met on *The Driver*. Gordon said that he could shoot a film in Siberia and be confident that Frank could line produce it for him, and he asked me if I would have the nerve to tell Burt Reynolds something negative if it needed to be said (Gordon had produced a Reynolds film). I replied that I felt I could, although I would couch it in a diplomatic, conciliatory style. Nothing came from that meeting, as I had the feeling that he was looking more for a line producer like Frank than a development executive like myself, but I was grateful to "Killer" Kane for the intro.

My other great friend and fantasy dream girl, Meridith, put me in touch with Michael Barlow, who had just received that credit that I had coveted, associate producer, on a prestigious film, a remake of the old noir movie *The Postman Always Rings Twice*, starring Hollywood superstar Jack Nicholson. *Postman* had been directed by Nicholson crony Bob Rafelson, who had directed Nicholson in his star making role as the intellectual antihero in *Five Easy Pieces*, featuring the famous scene where Nicholson throws a temper tantrum at a snotty diner waitress. Side note—I felt that iconic scene would have played more effectively if he had blown up at an obnoxious customer in defense of the waitress instead, but who am I to change movie history.

It so happened that Barlow was Rafelson's personal associate, but he was leaving to accept another job, and he wanted to make sure that Rafelson had an equally capable replacement. Barlow set up a meeting for me with Rafelson, and it went great—I was in awe of being in the presence of a Nicholson friend who had a reputation for intellectual filmmaking and perfectionism, yet I was confident in my ability to discuss projects and scripts given my background with another intellectual director, Ulu. After the meeting when I mentioned to Ulu's friend, producer Jerry Bick, that Rafelson reminded me of Ulu in that regard, Jerry cautioned me that Rafelson was a much "harder' personality, by which he meant temperamental.

I had a good feeling that Rafelson was going to offer me the position, but along about that same time, Meridith had completed her screenplay about the prison warden's daughter and was in the process of shopping it around town to make a deal for it. One of the producers who took an interest in it was Edward Pressman, who was to first time directors what Tony was to first time screenwriters, having launched the careers of such prestigious directors as Brian De Palma and Terrence Malick (who directed *Badlands* for Pressman after he had written the aforementioned *Deadhead Miles* for Tony). It so happened that Pressman had an opening for a development person, and Meridith, sweetheart that she was and knowing that I had fallen on hard times, recommended me for this position also. Her thinking was that I had a boatload of relationships with screenwriters that I had met with while working for Tony, and it would be mutually beneficial for everybody for me to transition them over to the deal making style of the prodigious Pressman.

I met with him, and was amazed to find that, like Tony, he was anything but a stereotypical fast talking movie producer, but rather a short, balding, bespectacled man who was so mild mannered that he barely spoke above a whisper. He mentioned to me that he was currently in post-production with a movie called *The Hand*, which was, true to his reputation, a first time directing effort by screenwriter Oliver Stone, who had written the aforementioned controversial David Putnam film *Midnight Express*. Pressman said that he intended to continue his creative relationship with Stone to try and find financing for another Stone script, *Platoon*, which was based on his experience as a combat veteran in the Viet Nam war. This sounded intriguing because Stone was not an uderprivileged kid who had gotten drafted, but rather an Ivy League graduate who had voluntarily enlisted in the Army to go to combat. Pressman said that he was also going to try and get Meridith's script off the ground, and he agreed with her take that I could bring some of my writers over from Market Street to possibly create opportunities for them with his company.

This sounded like exactly the kind of opportunity that I was looking for, and Pressman assured me that I would receive that elusive credit that I was looking for on any project that I was able to bring to the table. It seemed like a good match on paper, with me bringing literary properties to a producer with a reputation for handling directors and being a savvy deal maker, so we shook hands and made a deal that I would give it a try. I must admit that I was attracted to the idea of working for somebody with the easy-going personality of Ed, as I was very wary of working for somebody with a temperamental personality, which was a trendy trait in the movie business. I had seen my friend Michael Meltzer suffer at the hands of notoriously temperamental hair stylist turned producer Jon Peters. By the way, in the film *Licorice Pizza*, Peters' assistant is portrayed as flamboyantly gay. That was not based on reality, as I can tell you that Michael was decidedly not gay, as I know that he dated one of my female colleagues at Market Street.

I had also been concerned about Bick's comment about Rafelson's hard edged personality. Therefore, I wrote Bob a note that I was accepting the position with Ed, and he wrote me back a very gracious note telling me that I would do well with Ed, which really impressed me that once again such a heavyweight in the business would take the time to wish me well with no hard feelings.

I would be transitioned into Ed's company by his current development person, who turned out to be none other than Ron Shelton, the writer of *Bull Durham*! Pressman had hired him while Ron was trying to get Bull off the ground, and Ron was leaving to pursue his project full time, now that he had a well-known Hollywood agent, Geoff Sanford, representing him. As mentioned, Ron and I had hit it off when we had met at Market Street, and we then spent a couple of great weeks in the office together while he brought me up to speed on all of Pressman's projects, including an idea that Ron had brought to him about a music bio of Jerry Lee Lewis. Ron and I also chatted about Oliver Stone, and Ron characterized it perfectly. He said that they got along OK, but there was no affinity there, and I was not surprised because Ron had the friendly easygoing personality of the ex-jock that he was. Stone, on the other hand, based on the success of *Midnight Express*, already had the reputation of being somewhat of an enfant terrible.

Ron's final two weeks flew by, and then I was left to fend for myself with the remainder of Ed's staff, and it really was a case of what Jerry Seinfeld used to refer to as Superman's "bizarro world" on his TV show. Instead of the warm personality of Tony's assistant Wendy, Ed's secretary was a tall, no nonsense Nordic goddess type; Ed's finance guy was a slightly surly, not particularly friendly type; and Ed's right-hand guy was a veteran New Yorker who was friendly enough but not particularly helpful. In other, words, it was reality, not the fantasy world of Market Street that I had just spent the last five years in. Plus, I was no longer ensconced in Market Street's cozy beach offices, but rather right in the middle of the studio system that Tony had rejected, as Ed was successful enough to have TWO offices, a main office at Warner Brothers and another office at MGM in Culver City.

To make matters worse, I received a call from Marianne Moloney, the *Ordinary People* lit agent, to let me know that she had just seen an advance screening of *My Bodyguard* and that Tony had awarded me a "Producers wish to thank" credit at the end of the film. The result being, my whole resign in protest/disappointment had been for naught, as Tony had made sure to give me my credit where it had been due. I was consoled, however, by the fact that *My Bodyguard* turned out to be a wonderful, critically acclaimed, modest financial hit, so my gut instinct on my "baby" turned out to be on the money. Regardless, I was determined to forge ahead in my new position and try to find a project that I could sink my teeth in to. I will give credit to Ed for this much, however—he did recognize the value of announcing my addition to his staff in the Hollywood trade papers, and there was a front-page article in the *Hollywood Reporter* announcing me as a VP of Creative Affairs. I must admit it did feed my ego a little bit, and there was also a mention in *Daily Variety*, the "bible" of the movie business, so I could no longer complain about lack of credit—now all I had to do was live up to it.

The first order of business, as far as I was concerned, was to help my friend Meridith get her script off the ground with Ed, as I was extremely grateful to her for getting me the interview with him in the first place. I felt that the biggest contribution I could make to it would be to suggest casting for it, and I felt that I had honed that skill over the past half dozen years at both William Morris and Market Street. I thought I had just the right guy in mind for the role of the prisoner—Robbie Robertson, the lead guitar player for the classic rock group, The Band. A few months earlier, Tony's friend Peter Turner had screened a movie for us called *The Last Waltz*, directed by Martin Scorsese, and although it was intended to be a last hurrah/homage concert film for *The Band*, it turned out to be a spectacular showcase for Robertson. He was extremely charismatic, and the camera loved him, as he had matured from a young hippie type into a veteran, sexy, street-smart showman as the front man one for one of the greatest rock groups in music history. Meridith was a little skeptical about my take, as I am sure that she was hoping for an actor with a reputation, but I did my best to convince both her and Ed that Robertson was the ideal personality for the role of the sexy, sympathetic, street wise prisoner.

In terms of the role based on Meridith, the teenage daughter of the prison warden, an agent had recommended a young teenager who had already had a couple of leading roles under her belt, and I was introduced to her in Ed's office. She had a striking aura of innocent sexuality about her which I felt made her perfect for the role, and I told both Ed and Meridith so. Her name was Diane Lane, and that was a major disappointment to me that the film never got made with her in that role—she would have been perfect for it. Lane, of course, has gone on to become a female Jeff Bridges, and that is the highest compliment that I can pay her— like Bridges, she always makes a character her own, and always gives an interesting and dynamic performance with a high degree of professional behavior. My favorite role of hers during those years was as Matt Dillon's hot to trot girlfriend in *Rumble Fish*, a wildly stylized adaptation of a popular youth novel directed by Tony's friend Francis Ford Coppola and featuring a memorable percussive soundtrack by former Police drummer Stuart Copeland.

Ed and Meridith were also considering a young director at that time named Adrian Lyne and asked me what I thought of him. Well, as luck would have it, Lyne, a successful commercial director from Britain, had just directed his first film, *Foxes*, and because my aforementioned favorite producer, David Putnam, produced it I had already seen it, loved it and endorsed him enthusiastically. We met him, and he agreed with Ed and Meridith to "attach" himself to the project (meaning that Ed could use his name to try and make a deal with a studio). I contend to this day that the combination of Lyne, Robertson and Lane would have made for a stylish, sexy coming of age movie, but it never came together at that time. Lyne went on to direct the smash hit musical film *Flashdance*, and "Prisoners" was eventually made years later featuring Tatum O'Neal in the lead role. It was directed by Peter Werner, another one of Tony's young directors from Market Street, but rumor has it that he rewrote the script to its detriment. I would have paid to have seen our version of it.

Simultaneously, there was another project that I wanted to bring over from Market Street to Ed, a script called *My Kind of Guy* from the aforementioned screenwriter-director Amy Heckerling—both Warner Bros. and Tony recognized her unique talent and I agreed with them. That script was a great calling card for her in that it was an entertaining blend of wry humor and charming heart, and I felt that Amy's sensibility and great ear for dialogue would connect with a hip young audience. However, my friend Daniel Petrie, Jr., a member of the literary brat pack that we belonged to which also included screenwriters Jim Kouf and David Greenwalt and producer in training Michael Meltzer, had something else in mind for me. He had since been promoted to an agent at ICM and he had a project that he wanted me to bring to Ed that he thought was better than Amy's. It was also a charming romantic comedy, and it had the additional benefit of having a hot young actor already attached to it—Ken Wahl, who had given a breakout performance in the '60's period film *The Wanderers* and was being touted as the next John Travolta type, given his swarthy, macho, New York street charm.

Dan arranged for me to see a screening of Wahl's most recent film, *Fort Apache the Bronx*, where he co-starred with, who else, Paul Newman, so I could see for myself Wahl's electric sex appeal. Duly impressed, I then set up a lunch meeting for Ed and myself to meet Wahl, and his screen charisma did also shine through in person, he was definitely a likable New York street hunk. Ed and I were also impressed with his enthusiasm and passion for the project, and I hoped that Ed would add the project to his front burner of irons in the fire.

There was also another project that I had heard about while I was at Market Street that I believed in and wanted to bring to Ed's attention, a re-make of the film noir classic of the '40's called *Out of the Past* starring Robert Mitchum and Jane Greer. One of Ulu's close friends, producer Jerry Bick, owned the rights to it, and I became close to Jerry while he had an office at Market Street while he was trying to get another project off the ground with Ulu, a biography of corrupt politician Huey Long. Jerry had produced one of director Robert Altman's films, and he was such a kindly, professorial gent that I was naturally drawn to his warm personality (he had, in fact, once been a high school teacher, accounting for his knack of forging relationships with people, an invaluable asset in becoming successful in the movie business). Jerry believed in *Out of the Past* so strongly that he made me a fan of not only the film, but the whole genre that it belonged to, film noir. At that time, I was familiar with some of the better-known film noir classics like *Double Indemnity* and *The Postman Always Rings Twice*, but Jerry's love of the genre inspired me to seek out and watch as many of the films in that genre as I could.

Jerry also practiced what he preached, by that time he had already produced several Noir re-makes, including *The Long Goodbye* with Elliot Gould as Marlowe, *Farewell My Lovely* with noir icon Robert Mitchum and a British production of *The Big Sleep* once again starring Mitchum. Mitchum must have loved the fact that Jerry kept his career going long past his prime! I discovered my own personal favorite of the genre, *The Killers*, starring Burt Lancaster and Ava Gardner, which featured the concept of almost every noir: the "femme fatale" sexy bad girl who seduced the hapless hero into doing her bidding so that he then became the pawn who always took the fall while she inevitably got away with any money that was to be had as a result of their misdeeds. I must admit that ever since I saw Greer in Past and Gardner in *The Killers*, I have fallen for many a sexy lady over the years, only to have my heart broken in the long run—at least I have been street smart enough to not have to go to jail or suffer an even worse fate!

At any rate, I felt that the fatalistic story line of *Past* might appeal to Oliver Stone, and if he were interested, he could write and direct it while Ed could Executive produce it for Jerry as the producer, so I convinced Jerry to screen it for Stone and myself in a Warner Bros. screening room. Unfortunately, there were some technical difficulties during the screening that prompted Stone to throw some sarcastic barbs my way, but I think he was at least impressed enough with the outline of the story to see why I had thought of him for it. I am happy to say that while my stint with Pressman turned out to be short lived, Jerry was eventually able to get the movie made as *Against All Odds*, and the casting was as appropriate as could be for a contemporary remake. Our entourage leader whom we had never met, Jeff Bridges, was cast in the Robert Mitchum role and his character was updated to a temporarily injured pro football player, sexy Aussie actress Rachel Ward was cast as the femme fatale, and snake like James Woods was cast in the oily Kirk Douglas villain role. Jerry was also able to hire a hot director, Taylor Hackford (*An Officer and a Gentleman*), and *Odds* turned out to be a modest hit—it was entertaining, sexy, and suspenseful, living up to all of the elements that made the original so memorable. It also had a memorable title song, *Take a Look at Me Now*, performed by one of the premier musical artists of the '80's, Phil Collins, which struck just the right note for the melancholy tale of betrayal. Bravo, Jerry Bick, your perseverance finally paid off.

As previously mentioned, Ed was as much of a magnet for first time directors as Tony was for first time screenwriters, so at least I was able to meet a few of them. In addition to Adrian Lyne and Oliver Stone, I also had the good fortune to meet John Sayles one on one, and he was a refreshing dose of modesty compared to the usual egomaniacal personalities of successful directors. He had written and directed a successful independent film called *The Return of the Secaucus 7* and had every right to be full of himself, but instead he was low key, soft spoken and down to earth, a true pleasure to meet and converse with. If only all filmmakers had the grace and modesty of directors like Sayles and Tony Bill! By now I was starting to see another side of Ed, and though for the most part he was the friendly, soft spoken deal maker that he appeared to be, he also had episodes of introverted temper tantrums where he became darkly moody and unapproachable. I must admit that I was a little afraid of this side of him, as I was so used to the easygoing temperament of Tony at Market Street.

Regardless, I was determined to forge ahead and try to get a project going for Ed and myself, and Ed asked me to do a potential cast suggestion breakdown for *Platoon*. It was a Vietnam war script written by Stone based on his own experiences as a young soldier torn between the demands of two sergeants, one good hearted and the other violently evil. One of the suggestions I handed in was Tom Berenger as one of the sergeants, as I had been deeply impressed by his turn as the psychotic one nightstand for Diane Keaton in the disturbing hit film *Looking for Mr. Goodbar*. On a lighter note, he had also tried to fill the big shoes of Paul Newman in the prequel to Butch Cassidy, bearing a strong physical resemblance to the mega star, and I felt that he was on the cusp of becoming a big star in his own right.

Once again, I felt that I had a real knack for casting the right actors in projects, and I was hopeful that Ed would take me up on this one. Before that could come to fruition, however, I was blindsided by one of the most traumatic events in my young career—Ed called me in to his office and informed me that he was letting me go. To his credit, he went out of his way to be as kind as he could about it. He said that he and everybody in the office really liked me, but since the screenwriters had just gone on strike and there was no telling how long the writers would be out, he had to make the difficult business decision of letting me go. I was dumbstruck, as I had always taken pride in doing the best job I could no matter what the circumstances, and this was the first time that I was being fired. In retrospect, I have a difficult time believing that he could not afford to carry my modest salary during the duration of the strike, but on the other hand, he took so much pride in his own business acumen that he might have felt that it was the right thing to do in business strategy. I also have a feeling that he sensed that I had had a difficult adjustment from the fantasy land of Market Street to the cold realities of the deal-making end of the movie business, as was his approach, so in his mind he was probably doing me a favor by putting me out of my misery.

Ed extended a kind offer, I could set up shop in his other empty studio office suite in Culver City and keep up the appearance that I was still associated with him until his deal ran out there in a few weeks. As wounded as my ego was, I still recognized the advantage of keeping up appearances, and I gratefully took him up on it. I truly regretted that none of the recommendations I had made in the six months while I was there had turned in to a concrete deal, but I would feel somewhat vindicated a few years later. Another production company with Stone writing and directing made *Platoon* five years later, and Tom Berenger was nominated for an Academy Award, and won the Golden Globe, for his fierce performance as the evil sergeant who tries to win the mind of Platoon recruit Charlie Sheen. I can't say for sure that Stone remembered my recommendation, but I know he read my suggestions when I originally made them.

Chapter 10

I F***ED UP, I
TRUSTED THEM"

Well, here I was, back on the street again, but at least this time I had learned that I needed to get any kind of job I could get while I tried to find another position in the movie biz, and it appeared that the writers' strike was going to be a long one. Even though Ed was allowing me to use his office in Culver City, I was too broke to just try and wait out the strike, so I resorted to going back to the only other job I had any experience in, doorman-bouncer at a night club (not the type of hyphenate I was hoping for, like actor-producer). Fortunately, the success of the hit disco movie *Saturday Night Fever* starring John Travolta had inspired the openings of a number of discos across the country, and I was able to land a gig with one in West L.A. called Bootleggers.

I figured that the nighttime hours would allow me to keep looking for a movie job during the day, but I would not be able to last long at that pay scale—there are no tips for bouncers. I must give my friends credit, they came to the club on a regular basis to try and keep my spirits up, and I was even able to get one of my fellow former William Morris trainees, Neal, a job there as a bartender.

Another former trainee turned agent, my friend Bruce Brown, sensed how down and out I was, so he took me to the casinos in Gardena and played poker there most of the night, turning over his winnings of a couple of hundred dollars to me. It was really a sensitive gesture on his part, providing me some cash but leaving my ego intact. I was also determined to keep in touch with my other movie business friends even though they were aware that Ed had shown me the door. The first friend I made an appointment to see was Bruce Paltrow, the wise cracking writer from Market Street, who, as previously mentioned, had gone on to create and produce the cult TV series *The White Shadow*. I knew that Bruce's manic energy and insult humor would lift my spirits, but I had no idea that he had something else in store for me. Seeing that I was obviously down and out, he wrote me a check for $1,000 on the spot, and quickly covered up my embarrassment by joking "this isn't charity you know, I expect you to pay me back!" Remember, this is the early 1980's, when $1,000 was still a LOT of money, and Bruce didn't even blink an eye—it was the single kindest gesture that a non-family member had ever shown toward me, and I was overwhelmed by his act of friendship. I mumbled something about promising to pay him back and left his office with a whole new perspective of what friendship meant—it would also not be the last act of friendship that Bruce would show me.

Despite these acts of kindness, I continued to spiral downward financially, and in fact my life was almost a cliché of what it meant to be down and out in Los Angeles. I was behind on my rent, Ed's office lease in Culver City had expired, and I was literally leading the life of a starving actor who was not acting. Based on my resume of working for at least three industry heavyweights, I was at least able to get some meetings during this time. My friend Marianne Moloney, the Universal executive, put me in touch with an up-and-coming young producer named Burt Weissbourd, and I was intrigued by the possibility since he seemed intent on producing quality literary projects and had already established a reputation as a player when it came to purchasing the film rights to books. I thought we hit it off fine, but no offer ever materialized, and in fact he hired a true heavyweight in the business instead—Kevin McCormick, the executive producer of the aforementioned runaway hit *Saturday Night Fever*.

This put my job search in perspective, as I was nowhere near in Kevin's league as an executive, and in fact my ongoing search was taking so long that it came full circle when I was able to meet with Kevin also about the possibility of working for him as a story executive! I found him to be a friendly, sharp and accessible young guy, living up to his reputation as one of the "Baby Moguls" who were profiled in the LA Times for being movie executives in their 20's. I think Kevin sensed that I was looking for a bigger position at that time, but in retrospect I wish that I would have had the opportunity to work under his wing for a while and get some concrete experience in actual film production.

Another up-and-coming Baby Mogul I befriended at the time, Ron Yerxa, was an executive at CBS Films, and I will be forever grateful that he was always willing to lend me a sympathetic ear while times were tough, once even inviting me to breakfast at 6am at one of his favorite breakfast haunts at my beloved Venice Beach.

Ironically, I was also able to get a meeting with one of Tony's best friends, Harry Gittes, one of the producers, along with Don Devlin, of Tony's film *Harry and Walter* and also one of the producers, again with Devlin, of the Jack Nicholson Western comedy *Going South*. I was looking forward to meeting him, because I had heard many times from Tony about what a great and funny guy he was, and I also had to admit that I was intrigued by the possibility, as I was with Bob Rafelson, of working for a Nicholson crony. We hit it off, as he did turn out to be as funny and charming as advertised, but word got back to me that although he liked me as well, he just preferred a female for that particular position in his company, plain and simple. Although I was disappointed, it probably would have been a little awkward to work for somebody who was still such good friends with Tony, as my subconscious separation anxiety of leaving Tony had still not really subsided.

During this time, I had one more interview chance with a very prolific producer, David Permut, and he got the meeting off on the right foot when he joked that he had noticed my "thank you" credit on *My Bodyguard*. I thought that I would reciprocate by mentioning that I knew one of his producing partners on his most recent film, Robert Weiss on *Dragnet*, but it turned out that they had had some kind of falling out that I was unaware of, and the meeting was downhill after that. It taught me a valuable lesson about name-dropping in the movie business however—don't drop it unless you are sure that it will have a positive effect.

By this time, I had run out of both money and job opportunities, so I swallowed my pride, and asked Tony's former partner Ulu for a loan as well, and he was incredibly kind also, loaning me $750. Having to ask him for the money really brought my current plight into focus, and I determined that I would have to temporarily put aside my dream of continuing to work in show biz and get a "day job" in the real world.

Since there were no computers back then with job sites, one of the only ways to find a job was to search through the LA Times classified want ads, and one ad really caught my attention—the LA Kings hockey team was looking for ticket sales telemarketers. Growing up in Chicago as a huge fan of Bobby Hull and the Chicago Blackhawks, I had transferred my allegiance to the LA Kings when I moved to LA based on two factors. The Kings goalie at that time, Rogie Vachon, was my idol while I was a teenage goalie in a Chicago park league, and the Kings' radio and TV announcer, Bob Miller, was simply one of the best in the business. He was a genuine pleasure to listen to, and I had become addicted to watching Kings telecasts because of his friendly style which made him seem like everybody's favorite uncle. On top of that, the Kings, Lakers, and the arena they played in, the Forum, had been recently purchased by LA real estate mogul and notorious playboy, Dr. Jerry Buss, bringing a newfound glamour to both teams which had fallen on hard times under the previous ownership of irascible Jack Kent Cook. In fact, one of their most loyal courtside seat patrons generated the Lakers only positive publicity during Cook's ownership, superstar actor Jack Nicholson, who never missed a Lakers home game.

Dr. Buss was able to add to that Hollywood glamour by virtue of his own lifestyle and helped in no small part by the drafting of a rookie basketball player out of Michigan State named Earvin Johnson, The

Lakers were "Magical" again and became the sporting event in town to see, and be seen, by every celebrity in town.

The Kings, however, were another story, as Cooke famously put it, even the Canadians who lived in LA did not come to the hockey games because the reason they had moved to LA in the first place was because they hated hockey! Thus, the need for ticket sales people and I made an appointment to see the telemarketing manager, a big, gruff, bombastic, larger than life bear of a man named Fred St. Francis. I would later learn that Fred had a heart of gold, but he was an intimidating presence, and I had severe doubts about my ability to cold call businesses and pitch them the value of purchasing Kings season tickets. In fact, Fred put me immediately to work, and I was so discouraged by the experience that I did not return the next day.

However, after a couple of more weeks of hitting the pavement without much success, I returned to Fred with my tail between my legs and he put me back to work—desperation is the mother of invention, and I was desperate. Despite what I perceived to be the difficulty of the job, which was to set appointments for our outside sales reps to meet with the decision makers at companies, I soon settled into the daily routine of the sales office itself, which was simultaneously a lively and cut throat environment. Dr. Buss had installed one of his childhood friends from Wyoming, John Roth, as the director of the sales office, and although he was a kind, friendly and smart man, the outside reps were truly a bunch of piranhas. They were on commission only and there was a lot of money to be made selling the more lucrative Senate seats, which were a combination of Lakers and Kings season seats in the best locations of the Forum.

Fortunately, John was assisted by his wife Jan, who projected the no nonsense authority to keep the reps in check, and by Steve Dover, who was the son of Dr. Buss' other childhood friend from Wyoming. Steve and I really hit it off, as he was a super nice guy who had played football for Notre Dame until he suffered a career ending injury, and we spent a lot of time talking sports. Steve also did me a huge personal favor—he knew that I had become so broke that I was forced to sell my car, so he sold me one of his cars and allowed me to pay it off with payments I could afford.

In fact, there turned out to be a lot of perks in terms of working for Dr. Buss—instead of working at the Forum itself, our offices were in a nice office complex in Santa Monica owned by Dr. Buss. Since Dr. Buss was the social ringmaster at both the Lakers and Kings games at the exclusive Forum Club, he made sure that he rotated all his sales employees, including the telemarketers, into his private dinner table and seating box at the games, which was also celebrity studded. Since he also still owned hotels in Palm Springs, he allowed John Roth to host the sales office staff for weekend stays there; and, most importantly for me, there were plenty of comp tickets for us for the Kings games. Quite simply, Dr. Buss treated his employees better than any owner in the history of professional sports, before or since, and, for that reason, it was becoming more and more tempting to leave the movie business behind and enjoy the exciting ride that The Showtime Lakers had become.

I still had one nagging ambition in the back of my mind, however. It was becoming more and more fashionable in the movie business for actors to have their own production companies, like McQueen with First Artists and Redford with Wildwood, and I was convinced that I could be the project development partner in a situation like that, given my background at William Morris.

Once again, as fate would have it, I came across a ticket order for a past Kings game and the buyer was none other than Tim Matheson, the star of the mega hit Animal House, which had been directed by former Market Street tenant John Landis. Tim had been slowly rising through the ranks as a young actor to be reckoned with, including a role as a vigilante police officer in one of Mr. Eastwood's *Dirty Harry* outings. Mr. Eastwood had a knack of casting talented young actors early in their careers, including Jeff Fahey and more recently Jeffrey Donovan, as to keep the budget under control. When the role of Otter in *Animal House* opened up after Chevy Chase dropped out (good career movie Chevy),

Tim took full advantage of his big break and owned the role of the party animal/ladies' man/frat boy, including giving a memorable reading to my favorite line in the movie, "you fucked up—you trusted us!"

Animal House will always be remembered as the movie that made John Belushi a comic movie super star, but Tim's work in it was equally effective and hilarious. Once again, this was in an era before cell phones existed and answering machines were just starting to catch on, so when I called the phone number on Tim's ticket order, he answered himself! I somehow managed to finesse the conversation by mentioning my movie business background while also talking about our mutual interest in the Kings, and I thought up an idea that could prove mutually beneficial. I would try to give Tim the opportunity to become to the Kings what Jack Nicholson had become to the Lakers, its most high-profile celebrity fan. The equivalent of basketball courtside seats in hockey are "glass" seats, the row of seats directly behind the glass and boards of an ice arena, and fortunately for me these were not sold out for the Kings at that point in time. In fact, Dr. Buss preferred that the employees sit there during games as seat fillers rather than have them go empty.

I invited Tim to come to a game as my guest and sit in those seats, and we had a great time—he brought his agent and friend, Doug Draizen, with him, and we spent the night alternately talking hockey and the movie business. I was able to arrange this a couple of more times for him during the season, and then fate struck again. My two old buddies from Market Street, Bruce Paltrow and Bob DeLaurentis, were able to be reunited on a movie project based on the success of Bruce's TV show after the *White Shadow*, a hit hospital drama called St. Elsewhere, and they wanted Tim for the lead role of their romantic comedy script called *A Little Sex*.

To Tim's credit, he wanted to reciprocate for my Kings game invitations, so he invited me to one of his parties at his house. I was extremely grateful that he recognized that I was just moonlighting in hockey while waiting for the opportunity to get back into the movie biz, and although I had visions of *Animal House II* in anticipation of the party, it turned out to be a very civilized affair, with a guest list including one Mr. Bruce Paltrow! Bruce and I comically insulted each other, just like the good old days at Market Street, and I met Bruce's young son Jake. If I didn't know it by then, I was starting to realize what a small world it was in Los Angeles and the movie business, and of course Bruce talked Tim's ear off about what a protégé I had been to Tony Bill and how I had found the project that transitioned Tony from producer to director.

Tim then bestowed upon me the ultimate Hollywood invitation—he wanted to have lunch with me at Musso & Frank's, the most traditional restaurant in the history of Hollywood (featured prominently in Tarantino's *Once Upon a Time*). I eagerly accepted, and once again it was difficult for me to separate the dream from the reality—here I was, a sports team ticket seller, having lunch with one of the fastest rising stars in Hollywood.

Tim told me how he was thinking about starting his own production company, and how he even had an idea for a star vehicle for himself, a remake of the old classic film *Death Takes a Holiday*. I tried my best to stop from pinching myself to make sure that I was not dreaming and did my best to communicate to him how strongly I believed in his talent and how I felt that I had enough experience in the business to front the project development process for him. We parted ways with the understanding that we would keep in touch to see how the situation would develop, and I crossed my fingers that *A Little Sex* would be a big hit for both Tim and my buddies from Market Street, Bruce and Bob.

CANDID CAMERA

Walking in LA from 1974–2008

Selling Kings hockey tickets over the phone was a lip biting experience.

British bombshell Fiona Lewis of *Lisztomania* fame relaxes at Muscle Beach in Venice, CA (photo by Fred Hecker).

R to L, Notre Dame intern of Tony Bill, Mike Roth; writer of "Boulevard Nights," Desmond Nakano; and yours truly. The attire suggests a surprisingly formal occasion hosted by the notoriously informal Tony Bill.

Meridith Baer, founder of the incredibly successful home staging company, Meridith Baer Home, was the most popular party hostess in LA while she was an actress/screenwriter.

The Forum sales staff resting after a game of pick-up basketball during one of their frequent retreats at one of Dr. Jerry Buss' many resorts. Pictured at the far right in the baseball hat is Steve Dover, Joe's main ally and friend in the office.

Joe celebrating an LA Sparks WNBA Championship with actress Viveca A. Fox.

Although an LA Kings ring proved elusive, Joe did get to pose with Lord Stanley's Cup thanks to friends and hockey colleagues Bill and Tina Gurney.

Joe ensconced in Warren Beatty's former office, which was taken over by Mark Harmon with their deal at Paramount.

Joe and his brother Bruce at a Playboy Mansion party.

Brother Bruce and their Mom MaryAnn once again proved what a small world it was when they posed at a casino event with St. Elsewhere (and Bruce Paltrow) alum Howie Mandel.

Lakers Christmas Party with Kobe.

Although Joe worked for the Sparks at the time, he was technically a Lakers employee and part of the Buss family with benefits such as this.

Joe received a Christmas card from Elvis (and Col. Tom) while he was an agent trainee at William Morris for Clint Eastwood's agent.

JOANNA
CASSIDY

Joe thought he was dreaming when the "snake lady" from *Blade Runner*, Joanna Cassidy, roller-skated into his office right off Venice Beach.

Rob Lowe sent Joe a thank you photo after the Bucz brothers took Rob and his high school entourage to the Lakers/Celtics Championship game in 1987.

Rob Lowe starring in "ST. ELMO'S FIRE."

When the Lakers sold the Sparks, Jeanie Buss invited Joe into her office for one last (at the time) photo op.

Joe attended a screening of James Stacy's film "Posse" while reading scripts for Stacy's agent, Stan Kamen. There was a dark reason why Tarantino used the Stacy character in "Once Upon a Time in Hollywood."

Movie Star visits Carbondale for a day: Warren Beatty campaigns for George McGovern for President, with Joe (in the Easy Rider shirt) by his side.

Joe with LA Kings hockey Hall of Fame broadcaster Bob Miller at a Forum reunion picnic: Joe spoke the Kings Championship into existence when the LA Times published his letter during the playoffs stating that the Kings should "Win one for Bob."

Boys of Summer: Mark Harmon's attorney and best friend, Barry Axelrod, Joe, and Mark having dinner at The Spitfire Grill in Santa Monica. The guys smiled when Joe said that he wanted the picture so that he could say that he knew Wally Joyner's agent (Barry).

Chapter 11

‒‒‒‒‒‒⁂‒‒‒‒‒‒

ST. ELMO LAKER

I was now about to experience the truest of all Hollywood axioms, hurry up and wait—I was cautiously optimistic that my hockey relationship with Tim was about to pay off, but I had also been in the movie business long enough to realize not to count my chickens. Meanwhile, I was content to bide my time as a Forum sales employee, as I had been promoted to a level above telemarketing where I was to set appointments for specific sales reps, and one of the reps in particular, Bill, was memorable. He was raised in Orange County as a beach boy, so although he dressed in a suit to go out on appointments, he did not wear socks, but rather went barefoot underneath his penny loafers! Fortunately for him, Dr. Buss was also a notoriously casual dresser, constantly attired in frayed blue jeans, so he was able to get away with it. Bill was also incredibly glib and funny, and I had a suspicion that he might someday be successful as an entertainer, like a DJ or a comedian, and the future would prove me to be partially correct, which I will detail later in the story.

Meanwhile, Dr. Buss was starting to bring his children in to the family business, putting his daughter Jeanie in charge of two of the Forum sports, the LA Strings Tennis team and the LA Blades roller hockey team, and placing his oldest son Johnny, who had a reputation for following in his father's footsteps as a playboy, in charge of the LA Lazers soccer team. The youngest son, Jimmy, was content to hang out at the racetrack with his Dad and learn that sport from the ground up. This arrangement set in motion a sibling rivalry that was to last for decades as the children vied to see who would become the sole heir or heiress to the Lakers throne, and ironically, the USC educated Jeanie would ultimately prove to be most like her father in terms of her business acumen and savvy.

In the meantime, however, the Showtime Lakers, led on the court by the effervescent Magic Johnson and the slick cool mantra of player-broadcaster turned coach Pat Riley, had won the NBA championship in 1985, and showed no signs of being a onetime wonder—they were built to compete for the next decade. The city of LA sensed that the combination of owner Buss, player Johnson and coach Riley were on to something special, and the fans supported the team like no other team in LA sports history. This, in turn, created a synergy with the celebrity contingent in a star struck town, and the ultimate status for any type of movie or TV star was to either be sitting courtside within hailing distance of Jack Nicholson or to be firmly ensconced in Dr. Buss' not so private section of the Fabulous Forum.

The Forum Club restaurant and bar was also the hottest spot in town both before and after Lakers games, and celebs could be seen bending an elbow and mixing with the fans in the bar scene there, along with nubile would-be starlets looking for exposure and action—it was quite the LA party scene.

Back at the office, my hopes of reviving my movie career were slowly fading. A couple of Tim's post *Animal House* films, a bowling movie called *Dreamer* and my friend Bruce's film, *A Little Sex*, both proved to be disappointing both commercially and critically, and Tim's luster as a hot leading man began to fade fast in that fickle business.

A Little Sex was noteworthy in one regard, however—it launched the acting career of Kate Capshaw, who would go on to become one of the most famous wives in Hollywood history when she went on to marry super director Steven Spielberg. Although the reality of partnering with Tim in a movie company was fizzling, I still felt strongly that I had the desire and background to help a star mine for their own material to produce, so I started to handicap any other possibilities on the horizon.

There was quite a bit of word of mouth about the performance of a handsome young actor upstaging his fellow "Brat Packers" in a film called

St. Elmo's Fire. Since I took a great deal of pride in my ability to peg up and coming stars as the real thing or not, I went to go see Fire and the performance of young Rob Lowe for myself. I had to admit, the kid had charisma and sex appeal—he was incredibly good looking but projected a sense of self-deprecating humor to show that he did not take himself too seriously. Coincidentally, Rob was represented by ICM, where my old friend Dan Petrie, Jr., who had set up my meeting with Ken Wahl and Ed Pressman, was still an agent. I really have to give Dan credit—by that time the business had come to the conclusion that I had blown my big chance with Tony Bill so I was not on anybody's "A list" of viable employees.

Dan was a true friend, however, and he put me in touch with Rob's agent's office, and they in turn put me in touch with Rob's manager, Tim Wood. It should be noted that most stars, both male and female, had personal managers in addition to agents, as someone to guide them through the (hopefully) long haul of their careers.

Once again the combination of fate and friend had dealt me a great hand—Tim Wood was a true gentleman in the style of old Hollywood, and could not have been more gracious and charming during our meeting in a trendy Hollywood bistro. As hot as his client was, he was still savvy enough to realize that it was never too early to start thinking of developing your own material, and he respected the fact that my background was geared to looking for material for actors. In fact, he mentioned that they were considering a bio pic of Eddie Cochran, the 1950's rockabilly singer, and that literally was music to my ears as, thanks to Dave Edmunds, I had become a huge fan of rockabilly, both past and present. We agreed to keep the dialogue going, and I went back to the drawing board of what I was starting to do best—using my access to the Forum as a springboard to introduce myself to the stars who were also big sports fans.

As it happened, Rob was a huge Lakers' fan, and the Lakers were in the process of steamrolling their way through the playoffs in 1987 toward the inevitable showdown with the hated Boston Celtics and their trash talking star, Larry Bird. As previously mentioned, one of the best perks of being a Forum employee under Dr. Buss was comp tickets to Lakers and Kings games, but I must admit that I did not expect to receive comps for the Lakers' playoff run, it was just too hot a ticket. Fortunately for me, I was friendly with the young man who oversaw dispensing the comp tickets to the employees, and I have to mention his name, Paul Cohen, since he did me one of the biggest favors anybody has ever done for me.

Unbelievably, all employees were entitled to two comp tickets for EACH of the Lakers' three potential home games in the championship finals against the Celtics, and Paul, with Steve Dover's consent, allowed me to consolidate all six of my tickets for the final home game of the championship!

Even the LA Times had written that this game was the most in demand game, ticket wise, in the history of LA professional sports, and here I was clutching six of the priceless ducats in my very own hand. Even though the location was in the upper half of the Forum, the scarcity of them would reduce anybody to beggars can't be choosers location wise.

Now for the biggest parlay of my life. I called Rob Lowe's manager, Tim, and offered four of the six tickets to Rob to attend the game as my guest (my brother and I would use the other two). I warned Tim that the seat location was not befitting Rob's status as an up-and-coming celebrity superstar, but they responded as I had hoped. Rob was such a genuine Lakers' fan and any tickets to this game were so difficult to come by, that he gratefully accepted and would be bringing three of his best friends from high school with him. Tim also mentioned to me, as I had also hoped, that the game would give Rob the opportunity to meet me in person in terms of any future business possibilities with their company.

The night of the game arrived, and my brother Bruce and I met Rob and his buddies outside the Forum and then escorted them into the Forum Club. The atmosphere in the club and the Forum was electric, and, typical of young men in their early 20's, they wanted to indulge in a little bit of alcohol celebration in anticipation of the big game. When we finally ascended to our seats before the game started, the scene was surreal.

Here was one of the hottest movie stars in town sitting in the middle of the regular Joe fan rooting section, and hardly anybody realized it was him because it never occurred to them that a star would be sitting in the normal fans' seats (although we did get a few double takes from young female fans)! To his credit, Rob seemed relieved to be unrecognizable since it allowed him to enjoy the game as a normal fan would without having to worry about dealing with any fan requests.

As it was, the place was jumping with excitement and anticipation, and every Lakers basket was met with a roaring ovation of approval—I have been fortunate to have attended many championship games in all sports over the years, but I have never seen a crowd that was as into a game as that one was. By the second half, Rob was whooping and hollering with the best of them, and he and his friends even whipped off their shirts and twirled them overhead in a spontaneous show of ecstatic support for the home team Lakers. If there had been any women nearby that realized that it was Rob Lowe who was taking off his shirt, I am sure that they may have fainted at the sight!

The Lakers went on to win the game and the championship, and I was happy that I was responsible for Rob being able to enjoy it as a normal fan with his friends—it's safe to say that my brother and I were key members of the Rob Lowe entourage for a day.

As I had hoped, Tim called me the next day to let me know that Rob had indeed liked me and was excited that he had had the opportunity to witness the game in person. Not only was I excited that I met with Rob's approval, but I also found out that Rob had another film coming out where he played a junior hockey player, *Youngblood*, so I could be going to work for a star who was starring in a movie about my favorite sport! Even though I was already partial to it, I really did enjoy the film, and thought it was well cast with Patrick Swayze doing an enjoyable turn as Rob's teammate and mentor and Jim Youngs giving a touching performance as Rob's brother.

There were also a couple of surprise cameo appearances, one by former Chicago Blackhawks player Eric Nesterenko as Rob's father, and another by a young real life Canadian teen goalie by the name of Keanu—yes, THAT Keanu, and more on him later also. All in all, I thought it was a slick, entertaining take on the dues paying coming of age of a young hockey player, and it also had a hip, synthesized musical soundtrack as well—just a cool film on my favorite sport.

Now I was doubly excited to see what I could do for Rob's skyrocketing career, and then I got the fateful, good news, bad news call from Tim—they wanted to offer me a position, but not as their development executive, but rather as their personal assistant in the management company. Tim explained that they felt like they owed it to their current assistant to promote him into the development position, even though they did not think that he would last there long term in that position, and I could wait in the wings to take over the position in the future. The irony did not escape me that I had encountered one of the few honorable people in the movie business in Tim, only for the whole scenario to backfire in my face. Surprisingly, I did not have to think about my answer—I told Tim that, as much as I wanted to work for him and Rob personally, I just could not bring myself to go back to being an assistant after having been a VP for two of the most prestigious companies in town, Tony Bill and Ed Pressman. Regretfully, Tim understood, and we agreed to keep in touch if things did change down the road.

Once again, I was devastated, I thought that fate had sent me to the Kings and Lakers as a way to get back into the movie business for an actor's company, but both of my opportunities had fallen by the wayside. There were also changes afoot at the Forum—one of the employees there, a kind opera singer named Alexis, had gotten me a rent-controlled apartment in Santa Monica right down the street from our sales office, but the office had since moved next to the Forum in Inglewood. I was unhappy about the extra commuting distance and time, especially since I was no longer moving on to the movie business. Also, John Roth, the boss who had been so great to me, decided that he was going to re-organize the office, and he wanted me to become a sales coordinator for the other reps. His intentions were good in that he wanted to place me in a more secure administrative position rather than the volatile sales position, but he did not realize that I had no desire to deal directly with those volatile reps on a day-to-day, paperwork-organizing basis. At that point I was feeling extremely vulnerable, and I shocked everybody by resigning from the Forum—the disappointment of the Lowe let down combined with the new position penciled in for me at the Forum, were just too much for me to handle, I felt that I had to get away from everything.

Chapter 12

⚬⚬⚬

ST. PALTROW

At that point in time, I really did feel like I had to get away from it all, including sports and the movie business. I had just gotten my hopes up too high that I would make a grand re-entrance into the movie business by working for an actor's company, while chalking up my colorful years at the Forum as an interesting sidebar. The problem was, I was back on the street again, with no prospects in sight. Once again, I realized that I did need a day job to survive, as I really did want to keep my little apartment in a nice section of Santa Monica, but I did not want to return to the grind of the nightclub life.

In 1987 it was still not common to find a job online, so it was back to the want ads again, and an ad caught my eye—prestigious men's clothing store in Westwood called At Ease, next to UCLA, was looking for a Loss Prevention Agent, which was a euphemism for security guard. The aspect that appealed to me most was that once again it was a late afternoon and weekend shift, leaving me time to continue to pursue my movie dreams, and that it was a non-pressure job which would allow me to ease out of my current state of semi depression.

The manager of the store, Rick, turned out to be a good guy, we hit it off really well, and he hired me. A bonus to the job was that they wanted me to dress like a salesperson and greet people at the door, so they furnished me with a nice wardrobe that I sorely needed. Another pleasant aspect of the job was that most of the employees were UCLA students, so the environment was really friendly and low key, in contrast to the sometimes tension filled days of the backstabbing Forum sales office.

Rick's best friend Brett was also working there for him as a salesperson, and I hit it off with him as well, and I eventually became good friends with both of them, which turned out to be an unexpected benefit from what I thought was going to be a dead end job.

Despite this temporary reprieve, I still did not want to lose touch with the friends that I had left in the movie business, so I called—who else—my old buddy Bruce Paltrow, who by this time had segued from directing Tim Matheson's movie to returning to TV in order to create and executive produce the hospital show, *St. Elsewhere*. Like his previous show, *The White Shadow*, *St. Elsewhere* was a "dramedy," and was even more off beat than Shadow or your usual hospital drama. The cast was eclectic, including veteran William Daniels, sitcom star David Birney, comedian Howie Mandel, beauty queen Cynthia Sykes, acerbic Ed Begley, Jr., good guy David Morse and newcomer Denzel Washington, and it was an ensemble that truly worked.

I updated Bruce on my bad luck with the Tim Matheson and Rob Lowe situations, and that prompted him to say that he knew another actor who was currently on his show that he was sure would want a creative affairs partner someday, Mark Harmon. Mark had replaced Birney on the show, and in addition to St. Elsewhere, he had received great reviews for his performance in a TV movie about serial killer Ted Bundy and was also starring in a series of popular, outdoorsy Coors beer commercials. Although he had yet to make his mark in feature films, Bruce was effusive that not only would Mark become a feature actor but would eventually branch out to produce his own films as well. I was flattered that Bruce was sharing this take with me like I was somebody in the business who still mattered, and he capped off the call by saying that even though Mark was probably still a couple years away from reaching that point, he wanted Mark to know about me, so he would have Mark call me! Keep in mind that this is one of the most prestigious producers in TV telling a clothing store security guard that he will one day partner with one of the hottest actors in television—have you ever heard of anybody believing in anybody as much as Bruce believed in me, because apart from my immediate family, I had not. I believed that Bruce was sincere in his desire to continue to help me, but he was also so busy that I really did not expect anything to come from it. I should have known better—within the week, the front desk at the store paged me that I had a phone call, and it was Mark Harmon!

Mark was simultaneously polite and forthcoming—Bruce had told him about me, he indeed planned on one day forming his own production company but did not know yet when that day might come. However, he did want to keep in touch with me, and assured me that we would through our mutual connection in Bruce. I was flabbergasted—this had been the low point of my life career wise, yet Bruce refused to give up on me, and, in fact, was introducing me to an actor whom he felt had movie star potential. It was also somewhat ironic, as Mark and I are the same age, and I had been well aware of his career as the starting QB at UCLA while I was struggling as a walk on at SIU, and I really had kept up with his acting career given that former familiarity with him as a football player. Once again, Bruce had supplied me with the most important gift that one could impart to another human being—hope.

In the meantime, I was enjoying another dynamic within the store—since we were a freestanding store that fronted on a busy street in Westwood, our manager Rick also employed a few LAPD SWAT members and West LAPD detectives to moonlight as undercover protection in the store. I spent many an hour shooting the breeze with them and became friendly with two officers in particular. Jerry was a muscular, jovial SWAT officer who looked like the actor Ed Harris and enjoyed sporting Reyn Spooner Hawaiian shirts as his garb of choice, the loose-fitting shirt the better to cover his service revolver, and John was a friendly, street smart plain clothes detective who also dabbled in real estate investment.

Both men were so interesting that I truly looked forward to coming to work just so I could speak with them. I learned two things in particular—SWAT officers love to pull practical jokes on each other, and almost all law enforcement officers love to moonlight for extra cash. In fact, John was not only working for us, but he was also moonlighting as private security at one of the biggest investment firms in the world, Drexel, Burnham, Lambert in Beverly Hills, headed by financier guru Michael Milken. As for the practical jokes, one of the SWAT officers in particular, Pete, fancied himself to be quite the ladies' man, so his fellow officer Jerry and the manager Rick thought that they would take him down a peg. They had one of the female cashiers call the store while she was off work and ask for Pete, pretending to be a customer who had seen Pete in the store and was so taken by him that she wanted to get together with him. They arranged to meet in a restaurant/bar right up the street from the store, but instead of the "mystery girl," Pete found Jerry, Rick and his other fellow officers lying in wait to break the bad news to him that there was no mystery girl with a crush on him. Pete took the good-natured kidding in stride, but he ultimately had the last laugh—a few years later, Pete Weireter was the SWAT officer who talked O.J. Simpson out of the Bronco and more than earned his fifteen minutes of fame.

Amazingly, Pete was also involved in another notorious crime in 1997, when he answered the call for the infamous North Hollywood bank shootout. Fortunately, Pete survived that gun battle and parlayed his expertise into becoming a movie extra and technical advisor for films involving police procedures. Art imitated life when director Michael Mann of *Miami Vice* fame recreated the shootout in his now classic crime film *Heat* which brought Al Pacino and Robert DeNiro together in the same scene for the first time. Coincidental observation: have you ever noticed that many of the all-time great actors have a last name that ends in "o?" Brando, DeNiro, Pacino, DiCaprio and Franco—just sayin'.

Another one of our moonlighting detectives, John Rosenbrock's colleague Steve Osti, also was involved in the investigation in a local high profile murder case involving the son of Marlon Brando, Christian, and unfortunately committed a technical error which resulted in Christian's virtual confession tape being ruled inadmissible in the trial.

Finally, even John himself was victimized by fate—the top executive at his other moonlighting firm, Milken, was accused of financial wrongdoing, bringing down the firm in the process. Who would have thought at the time that our little clothing store would feature these good cops in such notorious local scandals and that I would be friendly with all three of them! By this time, I was closing in on a year of tenure in the store and had since become the manager of the department, during which I promoted one of the students, "Sully," from stock boy to agent, and, unbeknownst to both of us, he would be able to return the favor years later. Also, by this time, Mark Harmon's career was continuing to skyrocket, as he had chalked up three more accomplishments since we had spoken on the phone. He had starred in a teen comedy for Paramount called Summer School, so he now had a successful feature film under his belt; People magazine had named him "Sexiest Man Alive" in their second annual pronouncement (Mel Gibson had been the first); and he was being rumored to replace Don Johnson in the white-hot TV series Miami Vice during Johnson's contractual squabble. Not surprisingly, Bruce Paltrow had been right about Mark's potential, but I wasn't sure if the timing was right to try and interject myself back into the scenario.

Fate once again interceded on my behalf, however—one day Mark returned to his old stomping grounds in Westwood and walked into our store to do a little shopping! I had to make a life altering decision on the spot—I could walk up to him and introduce myself as the friend of Bruce whom he had spoken to on the phone, risking my movie business credibility when he could plainly see that I was a store employee. Or I could just lay low and give Bruce a call later, telling him that I had seen Mark but opted not to approach him in public. I figured that this stroke of fate was too good to pass up, so I approached Mark and introduced myself, reminding him that we had spoken on the phone earlier that year. Mark could not have been nicer—he said that he remembered our conversation (whether he did or not, I am sure that he at least remembered that Bruce had told him about me). He also said that he was glad that I had approached him, as he was currently weighing a couple of offers from the studios and was going to need a development partner when he signed up with one! As luck would further have it, his manager, Neil Koeningsberg, whom I had met back when his P.R. firm, one of the best in town, had met with Tony Bill, accompanied him. Even though I don't think he remembered me specifically, he could still vouch to Mark that if I had been an executive with Tony, my literary credibility was intact.

Mark requested my phone number, and he said that they would be in touch with me as the studio situation continued to develop. I was ecstatic over this mind-boggling twist of fate, and from that day forward I truly did believe in the power of fate as a spiritual force to be reckoned with, not to mention the spiritual force of one Mr. Bruce Paltrow! I tempered my optimism, however, given my two recent disappointments with the Matheson and Lowe scenarios, but at least in this case there was a real deal and position there to be had.

Neil did contact me shortly thereafter to let me know that a deal had been closed with Paramount, the studio that had released *Summer School*, and they wanted me to meet the executive there who would be the point person for their company, David Nicksay. I was familiar with Nicksay because he had produced a film featuring one of my other favorite actors, Mel Gibson in Mrs. Soffel, so at least that would be a conversation starter for us. I was relieved to find that Nicksay was hip, friendly, and down to earth, just a cool guy, and I was confident that I would be able to have a positive working relationship with him if I were chosen—at any rate, I was just happy to have the chance to interview and set foot on a studio lot again!

Apparently, things went well with Nicksay, as Neil called me again to set up a formal interview with both him and Mark at Neil's office right there in Westwood. I was as excited as all get out during the interview, even describing how closely I had followed Mark's football career, calling myself a "Quarterback Groupie," which elicited a chuckle from them. I did the best I could to persuade them that nobody had more desire to do this specific job than me, that I had the knack of matching up "sensibilities" when it came to actors and scripts, and nobody had a better handle on the types of characters that Mark could play than I did. I had not lined up anybody to recommend me to them, as I had in the past with my William Morris contacts, deciding to put all my eggs in the Bruce Paltrow basket and the fact that Neil knew that I had worked for Tony Bill. They let me know that they would be making a decision shortly, and I walked out of Neil's office with my fingers and toes crossed, hoping that I had convinced them that I was the man for the job.

Then a few days later, I was manning my usual post by the door at the store, and I was paged that I had a phone call—it was Neil, and I had gotten the job! I had to admit, already having had one dream job with Tony Bill, I was unsure that I would ever be fortunate enough to get another one, but here it was—I was going to be partners with one of the hottest actors in town in our own production company at Paramount Studios. Not surprisingly, I was simultaneously stunned and ecstatic at the news, but the one emotion that overwhelmed me the most was that Bruce Paltrow was the one friend who stuck by me and believed in me when I was most down and out. I also must give credit to all three of the decision makers, Nicksay, Neil and of course Mark, because it would have been very simple for them to take the easy way out and hire any one of the literally dozens of "D—Girls" (development people) who I found out after the fact had applied for the position. Instead, they hired a down on his luck security agent, but they all believed in me as a person and thought that I was uniquely qualified for an actor's company position.

I was very grateful to my friends at the store who had given me haven for that past year, so I wanted to give them the courtesy of two weeks' notice before I re-launched my show biz career. I was told that I was going to be the one to hire an office assistant for our new company, and I wanted to hire one of the salespeople whom I had befriended, Lori, as she was graduating from UCLA, using the same principle that had just gotten me hired—I believed in her as a person. Lori balked at what her position was going to be paid, but I nicely explained to her that it was non-negotiable and was essentially take it or leave it. I was disappointed that she decided to leave it, as I thought that it would be a fun position for her right out of school (after all, Mark was the Sexiest Person Alive), but I was confident that I would be able to fill the position still easily.

There was one more surprise left for the employees and me before I left the store—we were open on the morning of Christmas Eve, and who should walk into the store looking for me but—Mark Harmon! He specifically came down to the store during an incredibly busy time for him so that he could hand me a Christmas gift in person! That was one impressed group of store employees that saw Mark hand me that gift on Christmas Eve, and the gift was a beautiful Ghurka leather organizer, which I still use to this day. I would come to realize over the next couple of years that this was a typical gesture of kindness on Mark's part, as he is an incredibly thoughtful, generous and kindhearted person. That turned out to be the most memorable Christmas of my life, complements of the St. Elsewhere duo of Bruce Paltrow and Mark Harmon, a pair of saints in my book for life!

Paramount was riding high at the time, having just produced a couple of "high concept" mega hits, *Top Gun*, the film that made Tom Cruise a super star, and *Beverly Hills Cops*, a vehicle for fast riding Saturday Night Live comedian Eddie Murphy. Cop happened to be written by none other than one Daniel Petrie, Jr., my friend the agent from our Jeff Bridges entourage who had put me in touch with Rob Lowe, and it was also directed by Martin Brest, the young wunderkind from Market Street whom I had steered clear of. I really do enjoy it when great things happen to great people, and I was truly happy that my friend Daniel had not only made the transition from agent to screenwriter but hit a grand slam home run right out of the box!

Paramount was also known for their marketing muscle, and they spared no expense in announcing to the industry that they had landed a star of Mark's magnitude to a production deal—there were featured articles in both movie industry trade papers, Daily Variety and Hollywood Reporter, and I was prominently mentioned as his partner in both of them.

Another sign of their regard for Mark was the office suite we landed in on the lot—you talk about fate; it was the former suite of one Warren Beatty! It was one of the suites that was aligned with the other suites of actors' companies that Paramount had deals with, like Eddie Murphy and Pee Wee Herman (his office was a "playhouse") and given the size of our suite, I couldn't help but speculate to myself how many well-known starlets had "visited" Beatty there. Little did I know back at SIU when I was trying to get a word in with him that one day, I would be set up in his former office suite at Paramount studios as a partner of another movie star!

Typical of Mark's modesty, he wanted me to have the huge office suite while he would take the smaller adjoining office, but I could not bring myself to indulge in such a great status symbol, so we compromised—I would take the smaller office but would use the big suite whenever I needed to take a meeting on the lot. Once again it was the "is it real or am I dreaming" syndrome that I had experienced when I had met Steve McQueen or gone to the Laker game with Rob Lowe—I really couldn't believe that I had gone from being a retail security agent to setting up shop at a movie studio with a major star player. Paramount also wanted it to be known in house as well—they had one of their publicists, a very nice young woman named Jean Marie, write a feature cover article for their newsletter on both Mark and I, including photos, and I actually started getting double takes from employees on the lot when I would walk over to the cafeteria. I also heard that a few secretaries on the lot were moved to tears when they read my rags to riches story in the newsletter—I could vouch that it really was fairy tale like, complete with the happy ending.

Speaking of secretaries, I still needed to hire an assistant for our new company, which Mark had named Wings Productions, and I had the opportunity to interview a few candidates, including a young lady who had worked on a film, Permanent Record, with an up-and-coming actor who I was keeping an eye on, Keanu Reeves. His career was about to take off since his small role as the goalie in Lowe's hockey movie Youngblood, and I was sure that he had the sensitive appeal to become a major star along the lines of a star from the '50's, *Montgomery Clift.* The same candidate also thought that I should meet an actress friend of hers, Lori Loughlin, one of the stars of a popular TV series called *Full House,* and I happily agreed to have lunch with her—lunch with a beautiful young actress, sure, why not, I laughed to myself! Lori turned out to be a delightful young lady, and I was glad that I had the opportunity to meet her.

Another Paramount secretary named Monica Harmon (no relation) had been referred to Mark, and I think he liked her because she was savvy about studio politics, but there was just something about her that I didn't quite trust. I wound up hiring an aspiring young actress named Corrine for no better reason than that she reminded me of another popular actress that I liked, Shelly Long, the star of the popular TV sitcom *Cheers.* Typical of Mark's thoughtfulness, he took both Corrine and I out to lunch at my favorite restaurant, Lucy's El Adobe, shortly after we moved into the office. Since it was right down the street from Paramount, it was a popular celebrities' hang out as well, and I once saw Governor Jerry Brown escorting his girlfriend, rock singer Linda Ronstadt, through the back door.

Since this was still a time before e-mail became popular, Corrine's main job was to answer phones and input my handwritten script and book "coverage" into the computer to disburse among all of our Wings team members, including not only Neil but also Mark's longtime friend and attorney, Barry Axelrod. Barry and Mark had been friends and classmates while at UCLA, and there was no doubt that they were as close as brothers were, and that Mark trusted him completely. Incidentally, Barry was also an agent for baseball players, including my favorite player, Wally Joyner of the then Anaheim Angels.

To make the world even smaller, Mark and Barry owned a minor league baseball team in the same league as the team that my brother Bruce was the GM for, the Visalia Oaks. *The Los Angeles Times Sunday* magazine did a cover story on the league and the Oaks which mentioned that the Oaks were a family operated team run by my brother, mother, and father, while also mentioning Mark's involvement with his team in San Bernardino. This time my sports/movie business synergy was accidental but no less serendipitous—when my brother ordered his bats for his team, he made sure to customize the names of Mark, Barry, and Mark's nephew on to some bats as a gift to show his gratitude for them hiring me. Barry later kept the connection going by inviting me to have lunch with him and another one of his clients, Cubs pitcher Rich Sutcliffe—Mark warned me to look out for a hot foot under the table from Sutcliffe, but fortunately for me it did not come to pass!

Now that the Mark Harmon/Wings team was complete, it was time to get down to business. Neil had a backlog of scripts that had been submitted for Mark's consideration that he wanted me to read, but he also wanted me to get back in the swing of things by meeting some of the development candidates whom they had considered who had gone on to hook up with other actors' companies. These included Rachel Koretsky for Michael J. Fox, Kate Guinzberg for Michelle Pfeiffer and Barbra Kuhl for Meg Ryan. I also had to catch up on a couple of movies that Mark had already filmed since *Summer School*, one of which Paramount had high hopes for called *The Presidio* co- starring Meg Ryan and Sean Connery (my "buddy" from Market Street). Paramount had had good luck featuring other young stars with Connery, Kevin Costner in *The Untouchables* and Alec Baldwin in *The Hunt for Red October*, and was hoping for a third hit with Mark and Connery in *The Presidio*.

I was able to attend a gala screening of *The Presidio*, and who should make a surprise guest appearance at the screening but Dirty Harry himself, MR. Clint Eastwood! I restrained myself from re introducing myself as his agent's former assistant, but I must admit that I was impressed that he appeared at the screening—Mr. Eastwood was known to be personally similar to his screen characters, a lone wolf of few words. The reaction to the screening was good—even though the cop thriller story was formulaic, the military backdrop in San Francisco was different, Mark more than held his own with Connery, which is saying something, and Mark and Meg definitely made for a hot "Sexiest Man Alive Meets Sexiest Woman Alive" pairing.

Speaking of that *People* magazine tag line, Mark was due to make an appearance on the *Tonight Show,* and the show needed a copy of *People*'s cover story on Mark, but none of Mark's "people" had a copy of it except… yours truly. I had bought and read it while Mark was appearing in St. Elsewhere, hoping that one day I might have the opportunity to meet him through Bruce. Little did I know at that time that I would be handing over that copy to the *Tonight Show!*

In terms of *The Presidio,* however, the critics were not impressed, and the box office reception was lukewarm at best—Paramount didn't say so, but it was not the star launching vehicle for Mark that they had hoped it would be. Mark's other film that was released around the same time was a much smaller scale film called *Stealing Home,* and he had what amounted to a supporting role as a professional baseball player looking back on his adolescent friendship with a girl played in flashback by Jodie Foster. This film was critically well received, but had a hard time finding an audience as a feature film—in today's market, it would probably be released as a quality straight to video product, but at the time I considered it, to use a baseball analogy, a solid double for Mark's career and a quality feather in his acting cap.

At the time Mark did not have much time to look back, however, as he was embarking on his third film of the year, a romantic comedy called *Worth Winn*ing. It was one of the scripts that Neil had given me to read, and although Mark was not a fan of the script, he was interested in it because some big-name comedy directors were also supposedly considering it. I still voiced my reservations about the fact that the story revolved around a romantic "bet," which to me was always the kiss of death gimmick to try and base a story on. I was impressed with the sophisticated writing style of the female duo who wrote it, but I felt that the story gimmick was just too big an obstacle to overcome.

As the movie was still being cast, however, that didn't stop me from throwing my two cents worth in about the actress I thought should play one of the leads, a young actress named Janet Jones. I had gotten a crush on her in the movie *The Flamingo Kid,* starring my "discovery" Matt

Dillon, as I thought she was the ideal combination of sexy and sweet, but unfortunately, her next two films, *American Anthem* and *A Chorus Line*, were not hits, so she was no longer considered an A list young actress. She did hit it big in her personal life, however, as she soon became Mrs. Wayne Gretzky, marrying the most popular hockey player in the world, who had just been traded to my Los Angeles Kings.

When the directors fell through for the film, however, Mark had second thoughts about doing it, but by that time Neil had already committed him to it. The director who wound up being hired had successfully directed many episodes of the hit TV sitcom *Family Ties*, so it became a go project. Mark invited me to visit him on the set, and I must admit that I secretly got a kick out of being important enough to be one of Mark's "people" that were invited to visit the set. In my mind my first order of business was to introduce Mark to all the talent and projects that I had known of during my first half dozen years in the business. I also intended to get back in touch with all my friends who had since gone on to bigger things in the business since I had originally known them.

The first talent that I wanted to introduce to Mark was my former colleague at Pressman, writer-director Ron Shelton—I think Mark had previously met him, but I wanted all three of us to get together in a get—to- know—you way with the ultimate intention of working together. Like Kurt Russell before him, Mark had lamented that he had not gotten a crack at the role of the catcher in *Bull Durham*, as he himself had also been a catcher in high school and realized what a juicy role Crash Davis turned out to be. I think that in most decades you can identify the two leading male movie stars who were competing for roles, starting in the '50's with Marlon Brando and James Dean, the '60's with Paul Newman and Steve McQueen, the '70's with Robert Redford and Warren Beatty, and now the '80's with Kevin Costner and Mel Gibson. I felt that Mark should be knocking on that door heading in to the '90's.

I arranged for Mark, Ron and I to have lunch together, and Ron's initial greeting to me was "where the hell have you been!" Like many of my movie biz friends, he had lost track of me during my five-year stint with the Forum, but he had been considerate and thoughtful enough to invite me to his cast and crew screening of *Bull Durham*, for which I remained grateful. One of the main attractions of *Bull Durham* for me was the classic '68 Shelby Cobra Mustang that was driven in the film by Crash. Ever since I became enamored of the McQueen Mustang fastback in Bullitt, I had become a big fan of both the Mustang and car designer Carroll Shelby, and the one luxury I afforded myself with my salary increase was a new 1989 Shelby Dodge Daytona, which was more affordable than the Mustang.

Mark and Ron hit it off as I knew they would as a couple of veteran ex-jocks, but my interest was not only personal—but I also truly believed that Mark and Ron were a great sensibility match artistically, and that any project that we could do together would be special. Eventually, I came across an article in the *LA Times* about a golf driving range pro who tries to qualify for the US Open which I did send to Ron, but more on that later.

The next writer director I wanted to introduce to Mark was a member of our original Jeff Bridges "entourage," Jim Kouf. By that time in 1989 he and David Greenwalt, Jeff's friend, had several solid screenwriting credits under their belt, including *Class*, featuring guess who, Rob Lowe, *Up the Creek*, starring my old *Animal House* buddy, Tim Matheson, and Jim had since gone solo to write the enormously successful Richard Dreyfuss film called *Stakeout*. Similar to Shelton, I felt that Jim and Mark were a good match in terms of temperament, and Jim had a real knack for complicated plot structure that really paid off (not only *Stakeout*, but also the underrated *Gang Related* starring the late rapper Tupac Shakur in an atypical role of a corrupt cop with a conscience).

Mark and I went to visit Jim and his partner Lynn Bigelow at their Disney studio office, and they all hit it off as I knew they would. Mark has a genuine personality of down to earth, understated charm that is enormously appealing and makes him very easy to get along with, but he also has a side of intense, exasperated cynicism that does not allow him to suffer phonies gladly. Mark could also be extremely intense and combative when the occasion called for it, harkening back to his days as the UCLA quarterback when he pulled the big upset of Nebraska. I always felt that I did a good job of steering just the right people in his direction, and screening out the people with, to use an expression from the '60's, bad karma.

Another writer-director whom I had once been friends with but had lost touch with, Tony's friend Curtis Hanson from Market Street, also came across our radar when a feeler was sent to Mark about a project that Curtis was attached to. I gave Mark my honest take—most directors can be characterized as either an actor's director, or a technology director, and I felt that Curtis was a technology director. I qualified it in that I knew Curtis well as a person, and I knew that he was not temperamental or egotistical, so Mark would get along with him personally. Coincidentally, Curtis had just directed my Lakers buddy, Rob Lowe, in a movie called *Bad Influence*, which came out on the heels of a sex video scandal that Rob was involved in, so Curtis was becoming a director to be reckoned with (and my world was getting so small that it was microscopic). In retrospect, no director knew the Hitchcock suspense/thriller formula better than Curtis, and *Influence* worked on that level.

The project with Mark never came together, but it is one of the few regrets that Mark and I shared together. Curtis, of course, went on to become one of the best film directors in American history with *L.A. Confidential*, showing that he was one of the rare directors who, like Martin Scorsese, was both an actors' and a technology director. Not only was he an actors' director, but he had a real knack for casting unknown but talented actors who would become stars, like Russell Crowe in *L.A Confidential*.

Speaking of Market Street, I was anxious to reunite with Tony Bill, so I invited him and his new development person, Helen Bartlett, to have lunch with Mark and me at Paramount, and the commissary gave us the VIP table. I was definitely excited to show Tony that I had no hard feelings, and Mark charmed them as I knew he would—regardless of my respect for them, these were two pretty high-profile guys in the movie business, and I was determined for us to all work together. Shortly thereafter, Paramount coincidentally hired Tony to step in as director on a project called *Crazy People*, starring his good friend British farceur Dudley Moore, and it was a charming bit of whimsy with a cleverly sneaky script.

I also had not forgotten about my other Market Street friends, and I paid back both Bruce Paltrow and Ulu Grosbard for the "loans" that they had so generously fronted me. Bruce wrote me back a very kind, personal note stating that he knew that I would do well for Mark—once again, in retrospect, his foresight that we would be a good team was amazing!

In terms of the script pile that Neil had given me earlier, two of the scripts were projects that I wish Mark had gotten involved with but had already been cast. One was *Cocktail,* starring Tom Cruise as a (what else) cocky bartender, and Mark would have been perfect for the role of the mentor bartender, which went to Aussie Bryan Brown. Although it was roasted by critics, it was a hit, and I felt that it accurately portrayed the politics of the bar scene, a milieu that I was personally familiar with. The other script was called *Love Hurts*, by Ron Nyswaner (who had also written Nicksay's aforementioned *Mrs. Soffel*), and it was one of the most charming scripts that I had ever read. That role ultimately went to Jeff Daniels, who is a good actor but by no measure a star, and although it was not a hit, I still felt that it was a heartfelt romantic comedy (ironically, it was produced by Tony's former mentor, TV impresario Bud Yorkin).

Since Neil had given me those scripts to get an idea of my sensibility, I in turn gave him a couple of projects that represented my taste while I was at Market Street. One was a book about brothers in the Midwest and their romantic complications, and the other was a script that Redford had once optioned but did not make called *Great America*. I wasn't sure that the book was in Mark's wheelhouse, but I wanted Neil to know how much I liked it, but I did think that the former Redford project was feasible as a starring vehicle for Mark. Well, much to my gratification, Neil loved the book (although he agreed that it was not right for Mark) and he gave it to his other client, the head of our entourage that we never met, Jeff Bridges! It turned out that Jeff loved it as well and was particularly pleased that it was such an easy read. I wasn't sure how the scenario would play out, but I was pleased that Neil respected my take on the book enough to bring it to his client.

As for the Redford project, Neil and Mark agreed with me that it could be viable for Mark, but Paramount was not as enthusiastic about it as we were (the writer was named Paul Young, and Nicksay jokingly asked if it was the popular singer with the same name). Fortunately, we had what was called a "first look" deal with Paramount, which meant that we were free to take our projects elsewhere once Paramount "passed" on them. Since the head of another studio, Mike Medavoy of Orion (he had accompanied Sean Connery to Market Street when I met them), was a big fan of Mark, we decided to take it there. Mike's head of production, Marc Platt, met with me about it, and we hit it off, so I thought that there might be hope for setting it up there.

In addition to those projects, there was also an old movie that I wanted to screen for everybody that I thought could be remade into a vehicle for Mark—it was a John Wayne and Donna Reed movie from the 1950's called *Trouble Along the Way*. Wayne starred as a corrupt college football coach who must go straight in order to keep custody of his young daughter. I thought it was an incredibly charming movie that would have played right into Mark's strengths as a sympathetic father, but my enthusiasm for it did not generate much traction.

The idea of screening a film, however, prompted Mark to screen one for me in turn, and it starred his favorite actor of all time, Burt Lancaster, in one of his most memorable roles of his career, *The Swimmer*. A friend of Mark's, screenwriter Roger Towne (Robert's brother), had come up with the idea of remaking the story with the twist of Mark's character playing golf alongside his neighbor's homes, instead of swimming through their pools, as Lancaster had done. Golf nut that I am, I thought that this was an intriguing possibility, and we agreed after the screening to mull over the potential for this kind of heavy drama.

The other great part of my now high-profile position was that it was allowing me to be reunited with my movie business friends. Another member of our former Bridges entourage, Michael Meltzer had since become a producer himself after his stint with Jon Peters, producing a sleeper hit called *The Hidden*, and he approached me with a script that he thought would be right for us. I trusted his taste, and he was right on the money—it was a charming satire about a door-to-door salesman, and the writing style was right up my alley, so I enthusiastically recommended this one to Mark as well. I also had the opportunity to meet another writer that I had been a fan of, Dan Yost—he had written the charming off beat indie film *Drugstore Cowboy* starring none other than young Mr. Matt Dillon! One thing you could say about Matt—he (and/or his reps) had great literary taste!

So far things were happening just as I had hoped they would, except for a story idea that was pitched to me by a writer who was represented by a former William Morris agent colleague, David Wardlow, who had set up his own shop. I loved the story idea of a cop who has to go undercover in a kindergarten to entrap a bad guy who is the father of one of the students. During the interim of waiting for a meeting I had set up with Nicksay to hear the idea, however, they canceled the meeting because my former date's landlord, Arnold Schwarzenegger, had already committed to it! The idea became *Kindergarten Cop,* and it was a huge box office hit—that was definitely The One That Got Away, and I felt that it would have been right up Paramount's alley in terms of the high concept nature of the action comedy idea.

Then another bombshell dropped—Neil and Mark were parting ways! It turns out that Mark was looking to leave his longtime family boutique agent in favor of upgrading to a major agency, and Neil had paved the way for Mark to sign with CAA, the agency whose agents had split off from William Morris while I was there. During this process I read a magazine article about another high-powered agent that Mark was considering, Jeff Berg of ICM, and I thought the article provided some insights into

Berg's hard ball and literary style, and Mark liked his hard ball style so much that he wanted to sign with him! Neil felt strongly that Mark should sign with his guy that he was comfortable with, but Jeff *The Shark* Berg pursued Mark hard and won him over. I felt badly because I felt somewhat responsible for turning the tide in ICM's favor by giving the article to Mark, but Mark and Barry both assured me that it had been Mark's sole decision to make the change. I could understand the appeal of Berg for Mark, as he was the head of the agency, which carried significant clout in the small world of Hollywood, and it would be flattering to anybody to be represented by him personally. At that point Mark did not have any plans to hire another manager, as he was comfortable putting his career in the hands of ICM and Berg.

Both Mark and I met with Berg shortly thereafter, and it reinforced my original take that this agent also had one of the best literary reputations in town, in addition to his hard ball style. I was confident that it had been a good career move for Mark in terms of being considered for major projects going forward. Mark also mentioned to me after the meeting that he observed Berg listening to my take on one of the scripts we were considering and that he was taking my opinion seriously, which I felt heartened by. By this time I had come across another screenplay that I thought would be ideal for Mark and Paramount, a romantic comedy about a business woman who transforms a scruffy artist into a polished businessman.

Knowing how important marketing was to Paramount, I even hired one of Corrine's friends to do a mockup of a movie poster for it to submit to our Paramount executive, Nicksay. Maybe it was because *Worth Winning* had come out by then and had not been well received (although Mark gave a completely charming performance), but Paramount passed on that project as well. Now I was starting to feel a little frustrated that I was bringing good projects and ideas to the table, but it did not seem as if Paramount was that interested in doing any projects that were initiated by us. It seemed more of a vanity deal to keep Mark on retainer as a potential actor for one of their own projects that should happen to come along. In fact, the studio that we had given *Great America* to, Orion with Mike Medavoy and Marc Platt, seemed more interested in working with Mark than Paramount did.

As it happened, the trial run with Berg did not last long, and after a few months Mark signed on with another agent, a hot up and comer female named J.J. Harris with the newly formed agency InterTalent, headed by industry heavyweight Bill Block. At this point Mark just wanted to keep working, so he accepted a supporting role in a small independent film, *Cold Heaven*, to be directed by prestigious British director Nicholas Roeg. Roeg had once been an ace cinematographer for another British film director, John Schlesinger, most notably *Far from the Madding Crowd*, featuring aforementioned British beauty and Beatty flame, Julie Christie. The movie business continued to be small world for me, as Roeg had recently married Theresa Russell, the actress who had been friends with our Jeff Bridges entourage, and she was set to co-star in the film with Mark.

Being the Anglophile that I was, I was familiar with the author of the book upon which the film was based, Brian Moore, so I was all for Mark working with Roeg. I didn't blame him for wanting to do something different and work for such a prestigious director, but the role itself turned out to be a strange one, where Mark was reduced to virtually playing a corpse for most of the film. It was ironic because the literary pedigree of the film would have met with the approval of Mark's former manager, Neil, but he was no longer involved by then. Nor did I get the opportunity to be re-acquainted with Theresa, as the film was shot on location overseas.

By then we were also well into our second year of our two-year deal with Paramount, and I had the feeling that we were lame ducks just playing out the string of our deal. I was also hopeful that Orion would maintain their interest in us so that we could possibly segue into a deal with them—more than any other studio, they had a reputation for making deals with actors' companies, like Dennis Quaid. Sure enough, while Mark was off filming, we were notified that Paramount did not intend to renew our deal with them. I had mixed feelings, in that I thought that I had brought some good projects and ideas to the table, but Paramount had not even wanted to take initial steps to try and develop them. To Mark's credit, I felt that he had done everything possible to support me in terms of attending meetings and talking through projects with me, but he was more realistically fatalistic about what the real nature of our deal with them had been.

Still, I felt that maybe I should have done more to champion one project and try and push it through, and I was determined to get something going with Orion if given the chance. Fortunately, it seemed that Orion was serious about picking up our deal, so I was relieved that we would have a fresh start to get some projects going, including *Greatamerica.*

Mark also decided that he was going to segue into another project as an actor while we were transitioning into our deal with Orion, another independent film to be directed by famed Aussie cinematographer John Seale called *Till There was You.* Ironically, the former William Morris agent who had been my apartment neighbor in Venice had put the deal together, but we had lost touch when he became annoyed that I had pursued a former girlfriend of his. The way Mark described the story, it sounded like my cup of tea—he would play a musician who gets mixed up with a femme fatale in the scenic backdrop of the tropical jungle rain forest. It had a high budget for an independent film, and I was hopeful that this romantic noir thriller would re-establish Mark as a leading man to be reckoned with once again.

Our deal with Orion was in the process of being finalized, so I somewhat wistfully bid adieu to the former Beatty suite at Paramount and supervised the logistics of moving our office to Orion's suite of offices at their high-tech office tower in plush Century City. Although I had gotten a taste of the star treatment by proxy at Paramount, I was looking forward to a more substantial creative dynamic with Orion and their head of production, Marc Platt, the executive who liked me when we had met about *Greatamerica.*

However, I started to sense that something was amiss—although we had already moved our office into their office suite, we were not allowed to move in because the deal was still being negotiated. It was doubly troubling because Mark had already left for location, so I was left in a little bit of communication limbo in terms of what our status was. Finally, after a few weeks had gone by, Mark called me to say that Platt had offered to put me on the payroll as a script reader for Orion while the deal was still being negotiated, and although I appreciated his gesture, I declined for the same reason that I had turned down the Rob Lowe position. I felt that I had achieved a certain amount of credibility as a development executive, and I did not want to risk damaging it by taking a step backward, even temporarily. I should have known something was up when Mark was gently encouraging me to take the script reading position, and if I had known then what I know now, I would have.

Chapter 13

⸺⊕⊕⊕⸺

HOLLYWOOD HILLS

I spent a few more torturous weeks waiting to hear something about our deal, and almost two months to the day that we had left Paramount, word finally filtered back to me that I had feared most. Although notoriously hard ball negotiator Mark was unselfishly willing to accept less than his asking price to keep me and our company going, the deal was off. There was also no chance of Mark funding the company himself, because, frankly, there was no reason for him to, as he was busy trying to continue to pursue his feature acting career and did not really have the luxury of pursuing his own projects to develop. To say I was heartbroken would be an understatement—I had finally achieved my dream goal of partnering in an actor's company, and then in the blink of an eye, the dream was over. As mentioned earlier, I still felt that I could have done more to find a project so good that it would have had to be made, and I would later find out that I did, but it was too late to salvage anything at that point in time. Now I know why both Marc and Mark had wanted me to take the script reading position, but I was too devastated to even bring up the idea of revisiting it—it was over, and I found myself in a familiar position, back on the street again.

Fortunately, I had not moved out of my rent control apartment in Santa Monica during the past two years, so I was not overextended in that regard, but I could not afford to keep my new Shelby and had to give it up. The only advantage to my situation was that I had been there before, so I knew the drill—I had to get a day job again as soon as possible to survive. At least in my previous position as the loss prevention manager at At Ease I had picked up another vocation that I had a little job history with, so I set about trying to find another position in that field. I was able to land another retail loss prevention position, but not as prestigious as At Ease had been—the store chain was called Copeland's, and it was an athletic shoe store that specialized in offering previous years' shoe models at discounted prices, as well as the usual array of standard sporting goods equipment. At least it would temporarily pay the rent, and it was uncomfortable enough to keep me motivated to get back into the movie business.

Surprisingly, I was also offered another part time position that did not pay much, but which I jumped at immediately—two of my old friends from my days at the Forum, Jeff Shulman and Sue Carpenter, recruited me to be one of the LA Kings hockey game crew statisticians. LA had gone bonkers over the Kings' acquisition of Wayne Gretzky, the biggest hockey super star in the world, and now I was going to be perched in the Forum in press row, right behind the Kings' announcer who had made me a fan in the first place, Bob Miller!

To me, it was just another indication that somebody from above was watching over me, for I was at the lowest point in my life, and this chance to work for the Kings again, in an important role helping the coaches, was an incredible boost to my morale. I needed this positive distraction in my life, as the job at Copeland's did not provide the friendships that my job at At Ease did, and in fact was a surprisingly negative environment in terms of my immediate boss and his petty politics. I tried to use this as positive motivation to try and get back in the movie business as soon as possible, and I kept in touch with one agent that I had become friendly with, Monica Riordan, in hopes of hearing about any openings.

During my stint at Paramount I had also become friends with a fellow development partner, Suzanne Rothbaum, who was partnered with prestigious Irish film director Neil Jordan, and the warm and friendly Suzanne did her best to keep me in the loop of the business as well. Speaking of Paramount, I was interested to see that the secretary that

I did not hire for Mark and I, Monica, was in the process of suing the production company that she did wind up working for at Paramount. I was relieved that my instinct about her not being trustworthy had proved correct, and I wondered if Mark had remembered that I had dodged that bullet on our behalf. I am sure that she would have thought up some reason to sue us as well if I had hired her, in my case probably the suffering of listening to my bad jokes.

At any rate, the other Monica came to my rescue she had recommended me to a producer whom I had recalled as being friends with my friend, Meridith Baer of Market Street, because she was a female named Max—Maxine Goldenson, the daughter of Leonard Goldenson, one of the founders of ABC television. Max was working out of her home in the Hollywood Hills, and when I met with her, she laid out the position for me—I could be both her development person AND personal assistant for $50,000, or I could just be her development person for $35,000 and she would hire a separate assistant.

Once again, I stuck to my guns that I would not be an assistant again (remember that I would not do it for Rob Lowe's manager), so we struck a deal that I would work out of an office in her home as her development person. In a way she reminded me of a female Ed Pressman, as they were both heirs to rich and famous parents, so therefore they did possess a hardnosed business savvy, but were also somewhat unhappy and moody because of living in their parents' shadows. Also, I am sure that our mutual friend Meridith vouched for me, but in the hierarchy of Hollywood, the three of us would not be able to all be friends if I was an employee of Max. All I knew at that point was that I needed to somehow stay in the business, and I arranged with Copeland's to downgrade me to part time night and weekends while I worked with Max during the day—I had learned the knack of moonlighting well from my former law enforcement colleagues at At Ease. One bonus that Max was offering to me, however, was a percentage of her producer's fee that I would receive if I brought her a project that wound up being bought by a studio, and that appealed to me—I was still determined to be involved with a project that could be made into a feature film.

One downside, however, would be my commute—I had a gut instinct that I should move out of my Santa Monica apartment for a change of scenery, and I had moved into a room in a house in the hills of Palos Verdes with a panoramic view of the city. However, it now required me to navigate a twenty-mile drive on nothing but surface streets to reach Max's home (my instinct to move out proved to literally be a life saver— my former Santa Monica apartment building was partially destroyed in the huge Northridge earthquake shortly after I had moved out)! I was so relieved to be back in the business, even peripherally, that I considered this a minor obstacle to overcome. The upside was that I had my own little office separate from Max's house, so I could try to do my development thing in relative peace and quiet.

I soon discovered to my dismay, however, that the one thing that separated me from the pack, my script and book coverage, which had been praised by everybody from Stan Kamen to Tony Bill, was now rendered meaningless because Max had a condition which made it difficult for her to read it. Fortunately, I had one trick up my sleeve—there was a screenwriting duo, Kevin Mulligan and Joe Blitman, whose style I really liked when I met with them while I was at Paramount, and I had an idea for an original romantic comedy that I was positive that they could write a successful script for. One of my all-time favorite screwball comedies was *Ball of Fire*, starring Gary Cooper and Barbara Stanwyck, and I felt that I had come up with an idea similar in tone but with a contemporary twist to it. I arranged for Max to meet them, and we all agreed that my idea was worth Kevin and Joe writing a "spec" treatment for which we could then shop around town and try to make a deal for. Although my original fear that Max's moodiness was something that I would not be able to deal with long term was starting to surface, I did have faith in her deal making ability. I was hopeful that we could get my idea in development, that is, somebody paying Kevin and Joe to write the script with Max and I as producers.

As always, I had a casting idea for the female lead, and fortunately I had a connection to her—Meg Ryan, Mark's costar in *The Presidio*, still had her own production deal at Paramount, and I had become friendly with her partner, Barbara Kuhl, while we were at Paramount together. Barbara agreed to meet with us and hear our "pitch," which meant Kevin and Joe relaying the story idea to her verbally. I was excited, because by that time Meg Ryan had become America's sweetheart based on her popular romantic comedy *When Harry Met Sally* with Billy Crystal, making her one of the few "bankable" leading ladies in Hollywood, which meant that her interest in a project could give it a green light from a studio. Kevin and Joe did a great job of pitching the story idea in a humorous and charming manner, and Barbara loved it!

From my own experience with Mark and our production executive Nicksay, I knew the next step was for Barbara to run it by her production executive at Paramount, Lindsay Duran, who then had the power to put the project in to development if she liked it. This next step could take a little while, so I decided to strike while I was hot—I had another story idea, but I felt this one was more suited to a TV movie in scope, so I told Max about it. As mentioned earlier, I had grown up in Chicago as a huge hockey fan, and one of the stars of the Blackhawks during that time was a chippy, high scoring center named Stan Mikita. Although he was one of the best players in the NHL, he played under the large shadow cast by his teammate, Bobby Hull, nicknamed the Golden Jet because of his blonde-haired charisma and his fast, powerful playing style. Stan was Roger Maris to Hull's Mickey Mantle, and there was not much he could do to change his fate. One of my favorite childhood memories was being able to get both of their autographs, Hull during the pre-game warmups at an actual Hawks game that a neighbor had taken me to, and Mikita while I was working at a Chicago suburban golf course where he played as a one-time guest. That golf course was a gold mine for me—as mentioned earlier, I was also able to get the autograph of Brian Piccolo, the Chicago Bears running back made famous by the TV movie *Brian's Song*. My brother later worked for Piccolo's teammate and roommate in that same film, Gale Sayers, while he was a student at my alma mater, SIU, and Sayers was the SID there. I was able to frame both autographs for my brother, who is the biggest Bears fan alive. One more connection there—as previously mentioned, James Caan played Piccolo in the movie, and of course I was his script reader while Stan Kamen represented him at William Morris.

After Mikita retired, he did one of the coolest things that I have ever heard of an ex-athlete doing—he decided to start an annual summer hockey camp devoted exclusively to hearing impaired children. I felt that this was a story that deserved to be told, and my little fictional twist on it would be that a boy and girl meet there at the hockey camp and become friends. To Max's credit, she not only urged me to write a treatment for it, but she also demanded it. We were also able to contact Mikita through his business partner, and he gave his consent to the concept were we to eventually make a deal for it.

Then one of the strangest coincidences that I have ever encountered occurred while I was driving during my long commute on the surface streets to Max's house. I saw an empty building occupying a deserted stretch of highway right in the middle of an African American neighborhood in Inglewood, and the marquee for the diner/drive in style building said Stan Mikita's Donut Shop! I was simultaneously incredulous and perplexed—what in the world was it doing in this neighborhood? It was hard to tell if it was about to open or about to close, but it was most definitely empty. Now Inglewood is the city where the Fabulous Forum, the home of the Lakers and Kings, was located, so it would not have been unusual to see Magic Johnson's Donut shop, but a former hockey player for Chicago that I doubt few people in Los Angeles had ever heard of? That was really a Field of Dreams moment for me, and I half expected the ghost of the still living Mikita to come out and offer me a cruller and a cup of Joe! It could not have been because I was on drugs and was hallucinating it, because I never took drugs, and I half expected it to be gone the next day as if I was fantasizing it, but no, there it was, standing there empty every single day that I drove by it.

I couldn't help but became somewhat obsessed with this personal mystery, and I was also hoping with all of my heart that it was another incredible twist of fate for me, like Mark Harmon walking into At Ease. It was not until later that year that I finally found out the reason for its existence, so I just kept being mystified by it every day as I drove past.

Meanwhile, our meeting with Lindsay Duran at Paramount was finally set, but it turned out to be a bit of a letdown—maybe it was because they were a little nervous, but Kevin and Joe just did not have the same energy and enthusiasm that they had when they had pitched it to Barbara. We all seemed to sense it when we left the meeting, and, being the eternal optimist, I still held out hope that Barbra might be able to salvage the idea, but I was once again about to find out that show biz could be a brutal mistress. The anniversary date of my one-year contract with Max was approaching, and she decided to pull the plug on me.

During that time, I had a brief opportunity to try and land another position quickly before my contract ran out, so I did my best to connect with Johnny Depp's company. He had successfully managed to shed his *21 Jump Street* image with a series of dramatic feature roles, and his brother Dan was running point for their company at Fox. Their secretary did her best to try and connect me with Dan before she left her position, but I was never able to quite make the connection there. In terms of my stint with Max, I had mixed feelings about this latest personal rejection. In one sense I was disappointed because I felt that we could still get both the Meg Ryan and Stan Mikita projects off the ground, but that was another trait that Max shared with Pressman—they had no qualms about cutting people loose if they felt it was strictly a business decision. On the other hand, I was relieved, because Max and I really did not have the personality chemistry to make a long term partnership work anyway, and it did help me come to the realization of how spoiled I had been while working my dream jobs with William Morris, Tony and Mark.

And Stan Mikita's Donut Shop? It turned out to be a movie set for Mike Myer's "Wayne's World," Myer's tongue in cheek homage to his

Chicago roots and Wayne's ever present Blackhawks jersey as the hip hang out for Wayne, Garth and friends. It was always deserted during the day because they were filming there at night, and now the somewhat deserted locale made sense—they were far from the turf of any would be curiosity seekers. It seemed an apt metaphor for the ups and downs of my career to that point.

Chapter 14

⸻⊗⊗⊗⸻

LAKERS REBOUND

At least this time around I had a couple of things to fall back on to keep me busy while I continued my pursuit of one more dream job in the movie biz. I was still able to work at Copeland's sporting goods, and I was still doing the stats at the Kings games where hockey friends to keep my spirits up lest I get too depressed about my slow descent in the film biz surrounded me. It was truly bizarre, the Kings had been the Lakers ugly stepsister for so long, that it was hard to believe that they had temporarily surpassed the Lakers in popularity due to the one man show of phenom Wayne Gretzky. Now the celebs were showing up in droves at the Forum to ride his coattails and jump on the bandwagon.

Once again kudos to my friend Tim Matheson for being a true Kings fan before The Great One hit Los Angeles! Ironically, Copeland's had opened a store in Westwood in the same location where At Ease had been for so many years, and I requested a transfer there to escape my petty boss from the other store. The irony did not escape me, as I was virtually right back where I started before that incredible twist of fate of Mark walking into the store had turned into my dream job. It turns out that I had gone from the frying pan into the fire, as I did not get along with the store manager in Westwood either. My current lack of status was brought home to me loud and clear when Neil Koningsberg, Mark's former manager, coincidentally walked into the store and made a cruel remark to the effect that I had essentially gotten what I deserved. Apparently, he still held me responsible for giving that article to Mark about Jeff Berg that he felt led to his resignation as Mark's manager (Mark later told me that had nothing to do with it—they had their own issues which caused the fissure).

This made me realize that I needed to get a real day job again, as I could no longer stomach the realities of dealing with the politics of a low paying retail job while continuing to look for a movie job. They say that desperation is the mother of invention, so I called my old boss at the Lakers sales office, that kind gentleman John Roth, and asked him if he had an opening for me. My timing was good, since the Lakers had fallen on hard times after the retirement of Magic Johnson due to his HIV infection and the newfound popularity of the Kings, and they needed help selling tickets. I would be an inside sales rep specializing in doing the phone work for three outside sales reps who were offering combination ticket and advertising packages called Adpacs. The three reps were a lively bunch—Kevin was the crusty vet who had done it all, Matt was a young, hard drinking life of the party type, and Chris was the son of a famous novelist who was trying to make it on his own. The logistics worked out well for me also since on Kings game nights, I could just walk across the street to the Forum and don my stat man hat.

This lifestyle of Lakers by day and Kings by night turned out to be just the tonic I needed to suppress my movie business disappointments, and there was nothing stopping me from continuing to pursue any opportunities that might come up there as well. In fact, a personal opportunity came up even quicker than I had anticipated, but first, I always felt that there were three areas that I had become an expert in as far as evaluating new talent. I knew a great high school quarterback when I saw one (John Elway of Granada Hills High School in 1978), I knew a great young hockey player when I saw one (Mike Modano of the Minnesota North Stars), and I knew a great young actor when I saw one (Matt Dillon, Rob Lowe and Tim Matheson). Now there was another young actor who had broken through who had true star power, Keanu Reeves in *Speed*.

I mentioned that I had been following his career back when I was at Paramount and he had done the film *Permanent Record* there, but the movie business was not really taking him seriously despite a number of fine performances in small, independent, off beat films such as *River's Edge, My Own Private Idaho* and *The Prince of Pennsylvania.* The industry preferred to view him as the lightweight in the loopy *Bill and Ted* comedies and felt that he was in over his head as "I am an FBI agent" in the Kathryn Bigelow action picture *Point Break.* Well, when I believe in a young talent and bestow my Good Housekeeping seal of Karma on them, they usually come through and Keanu established himself as a movie star to be reckoned with in the mega hit film about a runaway bus, *Speed.* He was surrounded by savvy veteran performers like Sandra Bullock, Dennis Hopper and Jeff Daniels, but he more than held his own as fearless LAPD SWAT cop Jack Traven, and remember, I worked with SWAT back in At Ease, so I could vouch firsthand that Reeves was totally convincing as the supercharged hero. I had also remembered his cameo as the hockey goalie in the Rob Lowe hockey movie *Youngblood,* and knew that he had actually played goalie in the junior ranks while growing up in Canada, so was not surprised to see that he was scheduled to play in a celebrity hockey game before a Kings game at The Forum.

As I had learned by then, access is everything, and, as the stat guy for the Kings' coaches, I had a Kings' game credential which gave me access to anywhere in The Forum. I figured if I played my cards right, I could meet Keanu and give him one of my favorite books, the one Jeff Bridges had liked so much back when I was at Paramount (I thought Keanu was right for the role of the younger brother in the story of brotherly love). Everything went as planned—immediately after the celebrity game ended, Keanu just sat down and slumped against a wall outside the locker room to catch his breath, and we were alone for a few brief moments. I waited until he caught his breath, and then I told him that I was a Kings' staff member who used to work in the film business, and that I had a book that I was sure that he would be right for. I then held my breath, and he said something to the effect that his agents handled all his project submissions. I thanked him, and then tried to slink away as unobtrusively as I could before anybody realized that I had tried to capitalize on my credential. It sure wasn't the same result as when I had approached Mark in the store, but I really couldn't blame him—his attitude toward me wasn't dismissive, but he didn't know me from Adam and most performers are reluctant to engage with strangers for many liability reasons. Still, I was disappointed, as I really believed that he was right for that role, and I was hoping that my hockey credibility would at least gain his attention. Oh well, you never know until you try, and at least I had tried, but this time my creative approach went down in flames.

At least I had some real hockey drama to console me—that was the year, 1993, that the Kings went to the Stanley Cup finals for the first time in their history, and it was quite an exciting run. The city of LA was really hyped that the Kings were about to do what Gretzky had come to LA to do, which was lead them to their first championship, and the atmosphere was electric from start to finish, even more so than during the Lakers championships, as the fans were even hungrier for the first one. My favorite memory from that run was being able to speak with the late *LA Times* sports columnist, Allan "Mud" Malamud, in the press box before games, as we had the connection of both of us being friendly with Ron Shelton. Mud was not a band wagoner, he had been a longtime supporter of the Kings in his column, and I was hoping that the Kings could pull it off for all the long-suffering fans like the both of us.

It was not meant to be, however, as the Kings lost the momentum of having won the first game in Montreal when they lost the second game due to a penalty of an illegal stick used by Gretzky's on ice bodyguard, Marty McSorley. Of course, the irony was that McSorley was no sniper when it came to scoring goals, and the hockey world was perplexed as far as why he would have an illegal curve in his stick in the first place, but there was no doubt that it was the turning point of the series. Montreal goalie Patrick Roy shut the door after that game and the Kings lost the series, and they would not win a championship during Gretzky's stint in LA. All was not lost, however, as I was able to use my credential again to get a couple of Gretzky autographs before he left town, and I was proud to have my name listed in the Stanley Cup finals game program as one of the Kings' statisticians—now I had both a movie and a hockey credit to my name!

Chapter 15

‐‐‐‐‐‐

MAD MAX PART TWO

By this time in the mid 1990's I had comfortably settled back into the routine of being a Lakers sales employee, and as far as day jobs go, it was about as good as it could get, given the status attached to working for the Lakers coupled with how well Dr. Buss treated his employees. I was still even fielding the occasional feeler from Hollywood, as a writer whom I had befriended at Market Street, Barbara Marks, invited me over to dinner to talk business—her husband was Richard Marks, the best film editor in town, and he was considering making the transition to director. Barbara felt that since I had found the project that turned Tony Bill from a producer into a director, I could do the same for her husband, with the additional bonus of becoming a producer on the project myself. Richard echoed his wife's belief in me, and I was extremely flattered that once again a true Hollywood heavyweight was willing to go to bat for me. However, since there was no development deal in place, I did not think that I had the wherewithal to pursue projects independently on my own time and my own dime. I expressed my genuine gratitude to both for their belief in me, and I assured them that if I were to come by something that he might be interested in, I would bring it to them.

Another Market Street lady also tried to help me out during this time—remember when I said earlier that my leaving Market Street would eventually benefit the personal lives of both Tony and I? When I left, my protégé Sharon replaced me as Tony's development partner, and then when she left, she was replaced by a young woman named Helen Bartlett. Well, not long after Tony and Helen met with Mark Harmon and myself at Paramount, Helen went on to become Mrs. Tony Bill, and they also continued their film making partnership under the production banner of Barnstorm Films, so if I had never left Market Street, it is unlikely that Tony would have met his future soul mate. As for me, if I had stayed at Market Street, it is unlikely that Bruce Paltrow would have introduced me to Mark Harmon, and I would not have had my Andy Warhol quote of fifteen minutes of fame.

Apparently, Tony had spoken so highly of me to Helen along the way that she decided to try and help me get me back into the business, and she recommended me to an extremely important production executive at Warner Brothers, Courtenay Valenti. When I met with her and told her that I felt my niche was partnering with actors' companies, she in turn referred me to an employee at Mel Gibson's newly formed production company. I tried not to get my hopes up too high, as by that point in his career, Gibson had actually become my favorite movie actor, so once again it really would have been a dream job for me.

Thanks to a film critic for an independent newspaper, Myron Meisel at the *Reader*, I had really followed Gibson's career from the get go, as Meisel had championed Gibson's film debut in the kinetic low budget Aussie cult film *Mad Max*. Gibson's career then went on a fairly typical arc, starting out as the flavor of the month as *People Magazine's* inaugural "Sexiest Man Alive" based on the sexy thriller *The Year of Living Dangerously* with his Gallipoli director Peter Weir, and then plateauing with two box office flops, *The River and Mrs. Soffel*. Fortunately, Gibson broke through for good with the buddy cop action thriller *Lethal Weapon*, which allowed him to put on full display his combination of macho vulnerability and manic personality. He was then able to parlay this mega hit into a side career as a director, starting with the underrated *Man Without a Face* about a disfigured high school teacher. I was rooting for him all the way since, like Mark Harmon, I felt that we shared that common bond of all being former guilt ridden lapsed Catholic bad boys gone wild, to paraphrase a popular cheesy video TV commercial of the time.

I was really hoping that I had at least one bullet left in the chamber of my actor company career, but alas, it was not to be—it turned out that they did have an opening but were too far along in the process to consider a late contender like myself. As disappointed as I was, I still felt gratified that I had still had enough movie biz connections to at least be considered for these types of jobs, and I was very grateful to Helen for initiating the process for me. Still smarting from this "close but no cigar" call, I was stunned by the release of a new film reuniting Gibson's main competitor, Kevin Costner, with his *Bull Durham* writer/director and my movie biz friend Ron Shelton, *Tin Cup*. It was a romantic comedy about a driving range pro who tries to qualify for the US Open, and alarm bells went off in my head—after Mark Harmon and I had met with Ron, I sent him an *LA Times* newspaper article about a driving range golf pro who tries to qualify for the US Open! The article had really struck a personal responsive chord for me because while I had been working at my Chicago suburban golf course as a teen ager, I idolized the assistant golf pro there, Jim Jewell, and he had done exactly that -qualified for the Open as a club pro. Granted, a few years had elapsed since I had sent it to Ron, but the basic story concept was so similar that it had to be the same inspiration for the idea. Just like I know that Oliver Stone read my casting suggestion of Tom Berenger for *Platoon* but had no platform or reason to give me credit for it, my gut tells me that the *Times* article was the genesis of the idea for *Tin Cup*.

I have no reason to think that any malice was intended—I just couldn't help but think how things might have been different if we had all done that idea together back at Paramount. I will never know for sure since our paths have not crossed since the film was released, but as well as Ron treated me during my up and down years since we met, I would love to give him the benefit of the doubt.

Chapter 16

⸺⸺◦◦◦◦⸺⸺

WORD OF MOUTH

My previously mentioned comfort zone with the Lakers was about to come to a crashing halt, for in 1997, Lakers legend and GM Jerry West pulled off a personnel parlay that was almost unprecedented in pro basketball history—he acquired the reigning NBA super star center Hulk, Shaquille O'Neal, while also trading for a high school phenom from Philadelphia during the draft, Kobe Bryant. By that time, I had logged quite a few years in the pro sports ticket selling business, but I had never seen such a demand for season seats as there was for the Lakers when they signed larger than life Shaq.

It was the proverbial good news, bad news scenario—we sold out the Forum for the whole season within a matter of a couple of weeks, but we also sold ourselves right out of jobs—within a couple of months, the whole sales department of about thirty people were all laid off. I didn't realize it then, but I had managed to dodge that bullet—the Lakers personnel director told me to hang in there, that something else was in the works for me. A short time later, I was informed that the NBA was starting a women's professional basketball league, the Lakers were going to be one of eight NBA cities to operate a franchise, and my boss John Roth, my former telemarketing boss Fred St. Francis and I were going to sell the tickets for their inaugural season.

I had mixed feelings about this turn of events in that I was sad that all my fellow sales colleagues were out of jobs, but I was also relieved that I did not have to go through the stress of looking for another job. I was also still able to work for the Buss family as Jerry Buss' oldest son Johnny was going to be the president of the newly named Sparks. I must admit that I was surprised by the response for tickets to this women's professional sporting event, as it was just not basketball fans who purchased season seats, but women from all walks of life bought them as a show of support for women's rights to play professional sports. In fact, the atmosphere in the Forum for the inaugural game was downright electric—the people of Los Angeles welcomed the team with open arms and cheered them on wildly from start to finish, and the WNBA was born.

This initial success was short lived for me personally, however, as at the end of the first season, John, Fred and I were all told that we were being let go. Once again, however, that same Laker's personnel lady, Joan, told me to hang in there, they were going to try and find a non-sales job in the organization for me in the customer service department. As much as I wanted to stay with the Lakers, however, I was honest with them and told them that I just didn't feel that my computer skills were up to par for that job (I had none), so I was going to try and get another sports ticket selling job with another team.

This is where Johnny Buss stepped up big time, as he was just as surprised as we were when we got the news, since we had sold a lot of tickets for him. He then personally arranged with Joann Klonowski, the CEO of the new minor league hockey team, the Long Beach Ice Dogs, to get a ticket sales position for me there. Ironically, the owner of the Ice Dogs was one Barry Kemp, whose hit TV show *Coach* was produced by MTM, the same company that produced Bruce Paltrow's shows, so I felt a little bit of a psychic connection there. My belief in this connection came full circle when along about this same time I received a blast from the past—Mark Harmon called me out of the blue to let me know that he was referring me for a job possibility! About seven years had elapsed since our deal had ended at Paramount, so I was pleasantly surprised that he was making the effort to reach out to me, especially since my movie career had pretty much come to a dead end. The opportunity that he was presenting was a juicy one to boot—Mark and his lawyer/best friend

Barry Axelrod were friends with big time Hollywood producer Frank Marshall, Stephen Spielberg's producer, he had an opening for a project development executive with his company, and Mark and Barry had highly recommended me to him.

I was truly excited about this possibility since, as mentioned earlier, I had met Frank all those years ago on the set of *The Driver* while he was the production manager, had been impressed with his ability and friendly demeanor, and even interviewed for his job after he left Larry Gordon. He carved out such a good reputation for himself that he eventually became Stephen Spielberg's producer, while also producing his own films on the side with his wife Kathleen Kennedy for their company Kennedy/Marshall.

His office set an appointment for me to meet with him at his office in Santa Monica and being a big believer in killing two birds with one stone, I also arranged to meet with my friendly acquaintance from my Paramount years, Kate Guinzburg. She was still Michelle Pfeiffer's production partner, and their office was in Santa Monica, my old former stomping grounds, not far from Frank's office. I knew that Kate had good taste, for in her former position as a partner for big time producer Laura Ziskin, she had recommended my pet project, the book about brotherly love that Jeff Bridges had liked so much and the one which I had tried to hand off to Keanu Reeves while he was still in his goalie pads.

While meeting with Kate, she mentioned that they were looking for a director for their latest project, which was a heavy drama. I immediately recommended that she consider my mentor from Market Street, Ulu Grosbard, and I got her attention when I thought I cleverly characterized him as "Robert De Niro's second favorite director," as everybody knew that Martin Scorsese was obviously De Niro's favorite. De Niro had done two films with Ulu, True Confessions, and they also did a film together co-starring Meryl Streep called *Falling in Love*. I knew that Pfeiffer and Streep were constantly competing for the same roles, so mentioning a director that Streep had worked with would get her attention. I added that I was positive that Pfeiffer's experience with Ulu would be the best that she had ever had with a director, period. Kate kept a pretty good poker face, but I could tell that she was intrigued by my suggestion and the meeting ended on a friendly note to stay in touch.

I proceeded down the street to Frank's office, and the meeting could not have gone better—I reminded him that we had met on *The Driver*, and we just shot the breeze about the business for about a half an hour. He was as friendly and engaging as I had remembered him, and if anybody in this town had reason to let fame go to his head, it was he, but he was still as down to earth as ever. Frank promised to let me know his choice for the position in a timely manner, and I floated out of his office on Cloud Nine—I was convinced that we had hit it off famously, and that he would choose me for the position. I returned home later that day to find a message on my answering machine from Mark, and he was almost giddy—he had spoken to Frank, Frank had liked me tremendously, and I could tell from Mark's voice that he thought I was going to get the job. Once again, I was amazed that I was the subject of conversation amongst such industry heavyweights, but this time I felt that I had paid my dues and was ready for this high-profile position—I should have known that it was not going to be that easy.

Chapter 17

⌘

CHICAGO HOPE

Well, I waited... and waited... and waited—nothing from Frank. I had already been fantasizing to myself how I was going to give my notice to the Ice Dogs so that owner Barry Kemp would be impressed, and he and his fellow MTM producer Bruce Paltrow could joke about how an important movie executive like myself had been moonlighting as a minor league hockey ticket salesperson. I never heard back from Frank or Mark and a few weeks later I finally read why in Daily Variety—Frank's deal with Disney had not been renewed, so not only was he not going to add any staff, but he might also have to let some go in their transition to a new studio deal.

As you can tell by now, I am not usually a "woe is me" type of person, but this time I really had to curse my fate. Mark had done a great job of paving the way for me to have a soft landing back in the business, only for me to be stymied by the ongoing politics of the movie business and the fickle nature of studio deals. I had learned the hard way several times by then that when you had a studio deal you were on easy street, when you did not you were just on the street.

By this time, I was having serious doubts that I would ever get back in the business, and I had to face the reality of trying to continue to make a living, as my Ice Dogs paycheck was not proving to be sufficient. That's when Johnny Buss, the president of the Sparks, once again rode to my rescue—the Sparks had not done too well in their second season without a ticket sales staff, and he had persuaded the powers that be that they needed me back. My old colleague and former boss at the Lakers, Fred, decided not to return, so I recruited by colleague and buddy from the Ice Dogs, Patti Freund, to return to the Sparks with me. At least now I was able to scratch out a living again, and I was technically considered a Lakers employee again with all the matching benefits. One final painful revelation sprung up to remind me what could have been in the movie business later that year—*The Deep End of the Ocean,* starring Michelle Pfeiffer and produced by Kate Guinzburg, was released to rave critical reviews. The director? Ulu Grosbard, "Robert De Niro's second favorite director."

Convinced that that was the final anonymous exclamation point to the end of my movie career, I decided to focus in on my current position with the Sparks and try to repay Johnny Buss' faith in me. At that time in 1999, the Sparks, Lakers and Kings all still played in the old Fabulous Forum, but there was change in the offing—a reclusive Colorado billionaire, Phillip Anschutz, made Dr. Buss an offer he could not refuse. Anschutz would purchase the Kings from their current troubled ownership group and build a brand-new arena in the heart of downtown LA in exchange for the opportunity to purchase a minority interest in the Lakers. I am sure that Dr. Buss was reluctant to leave the Forum and all of his fond memories there behind, but shrewd businessperson that he was, he recognized the need to move into a modern facility and all of the new revenue that would follow, so he struck the deal. Anschutz would not only build the arena, but he also planned to build an adjoining entertainment complex, LA Live, that everybody hoped would revive a moribund downtown LA night life.

Speaking of the Kings, I no longer did the stats for them since they had converted to a computer system that was run by the league instead of the team, but I was still a huge hockey fan and attended as many of their games as I could. By this time in my life, in my late '40's, I had become a big believer in fate both good (Mark Harmon walking into At Ease) and bad (Orion Pictures going out of business after we thought we had a deal with them). Now the good kind was about to strike again—who should I see working the ticket sales kiosk at a Kings game but my old buddy Sully, Tim Sullivan, the stock boy from At Ease whom I had promoted to security! We had lost touch after so many years, and we were both blown away by the coincidence of running into each other at the game. Although I was working for the Sparks, Tim remembered (and I reminded him) what a big Kings fan I was, and he said that he would look into the possibility of bringing me back to the Kings under the new ownership group as an inside sales executive. Although I was happy being a Lakers employee with the Sparks, my heart was with hockey and the siren call of returning to hockey in a brand-new arena and working with a good friend was too tempting to resist, and I returned to the Kings after the completion of the Sparks season in the fall of 1999.

It was an exciting time—although the Kings had struggled both on and off the ice since the departure of Wayne Gretzky, the promise of a new arena and a new front office lead by Anschutz' dynamic first lieutenant, Tim Liewicke, the fans had good reason for hope for the first time in years. That surge in optimism translated into ticket sales, and I was right in my wheelhouse, urging the fans that their reasons for hope were not unfounded. I also had to admit that I had missed the camaraderie of working in a big sports sales' office, and working alongside a friend like Sully, who is truly a good guy, made it that much more fun.

Just when I thought the rest of my career was going to be tied to the Kings, that fickle mistress of fate struck again. One of my colleagues from the Forum in the early '90's, Chris Saul, happened to be visiting the set of a TV hospital drama called *Chicago Hope,* and he was introduced to one of its stars...Mark Harmon! It turns out that I had mentioned to Chris at one point that I had been partners with Mark, so he mentioned to Mark that he had worked with me at the Lakers. By that time Mark had pretty much returned to TV full time, and, like his days at *St. Elsewhere,* he had come full circle to be the member of an ensemble cast in a hospital drama. To further the coincidence, Hope was produced by Michael (not Ed) Pressman, whom I had come to know briefly while he had directed the Latino gang drama *Boulevard Nights* for Tony Bill (where I had refused a credit because I hadn't felt like I had contributed to the project).

Well turnabout is fair play, so Michael had hired Tony to direct an episode of Hope, and although Mark was not in that episode, he still came to the set to watch Tony in action. Both Mark and Tony remembered that I had brought them together for lunch at Paramount, and apparently, I became a topic of conversation between them that day. Fortunately, I had made a point of updating my contact information with Tony's assistant, Karen Svobodny, along the way, so Tony called me at the Kings and asked me if I could meet with him. I was truly ecstatic that my former mentor had reached out to me, and how ironic that it happened because of his chance meeting with Mark, whom I am sure felt badly that the situation with Frank Marshall had not worked out.

By that time Tony had fulfilled another one of his dreams by partnering with Dudley Moore and Liza Minelli (I told you Tony knew everybody), and opening a restaurant, 72 Market Street, right across the street from his production building. It had quickly become one of the hottest movie business meeting places in town, with the irrepressible Moore spontaneously pounding out show tunes at the restaurant piano. Tony invited me to meet him there for drinks, and I couldn't help but hope that maybe I had one last chance to grab the Hollywood brass ring. Ironically, what Tony had in mind for me hearkened back to our original relationship at Market Street. He wanted me to read and cover all the books that had been submitted to him over the past few months on a free-lance basis, with the important caveat that I would be attached to any project that I recommended which actually became a film. My feelings were slightly mixed as I had envisioned returning to my former status at Market Street as a salaried development executive, but on the other hand if I did find and recommend something worthwhile, I could fulfill my own dream of becoming a producer. Since we both had the desire to work together again on some basis, we struck a deal that I would give it a whirl, and I was still heartened by the fact that I would be returning to the individual and company that I was most emotionally attached to, Tony Bill and Market Street. It was also ironic that the name of the TV show that had brought us back together was my hometown, *Chicago Hope*.

I wanted as much time as possible to pursue this new path, so I resigned from the Kings to return to the Sparks, since the Sparks short summer season would give me a longer off-season to devote to covering the books for Tony. It also worked out that coincidentally Sully was also leaving the Kings to pursue another career path, so I did not have to feel guilty that I was leaving him in the lurch as well. At least we had both gotten the new Staples Center off to a flying start in terms of ticket sales and had been able to rekindle our friendship after a lengthy hiatus. At this time, my father was dying, but he was able to understand that I was going back to work for Tony, which pleased him since he always got a kick out of Tony's connection to Sinatra. I now went about attacking my new task with zeal, determined to find a book amidst Tony's pile that would reunite us as production partners. The strategy of working for the Sparks by day and reading Tony's books by night and weekends worked out well enough, but I just did not find anything that jumped out at me as a must do project, like *Ordinary People* had. I did take the opportunity to try and revive the two books that I already knew and loved the book about brotherly love that Jeff Bridges had loved and that I had tried to give to Keanu, and a crime thriller set in LA and Vegas that was a throwback to my beloved film noir. I thought I had read somewhere along the way that Tony had been interested in the brother book while Laura Ziskin and Kate Guinzburg owned the rights, but he had Karen send it back to me with no comment, which I knew meant that it was in his words, "a dead soldier."

We did meet about the crime thriller, and Tony observed that the spare style was reminiscent of another crime novelist master, Jim Thompson, who Tony once knew, but we didn't take any steps to act upon it. Once the book pile was gone, which took about a year, the position just kind of evaporated, but the upside was that it had revived and cemented our relationship going forward. Tony, his wife and partner Helen, and their assistant Karen went to great lengths to make sure to invite me to screenings of Tony's projects where he was a director for hire. One of those, *Harlan County War* starring Holly Hunter, received a rating of 9 from TV

Guide, the highest rating of a TV movie that I had ever seen in all my years of reading the Guide's reviews. I still read movie and TV reviews voraciously, thanks to the habit started in the early days of Roger Ebert and the *Sun Times* reviews, and the *LA Times* reviewer, Kenneth Turan, fulfilled my need there.

Fortunately, I still had my full time job with the Sparks to fall back on, and the team had, surprisingly, become quite successful, with a move to Staples Center and a couple of championships under our belt. There was a nice synergy between the Sparks and the Lakers, with Shaquille O'Neal even appearing at one of our games the day after he had led the Lakers to a championship! Because of this, I was able to make enough of a living to get by with the additional benefits and status of still being considered a Lakers employee.

Also, since our offices were in the same building where the Kings practice rinks were, I was still able to keep tabs on my favorite sport, and the Kings GM and former player, Dave Taylor, even asked me if he could join me for lunch while I was sitting in the rink lunch area! I was also able to befriend former Kings player and current radio color analyst Daryl Evans, who had scored the most famous goal in Kings history, the overtime winner in *The Miracle on Manchester*, when the Kings fought back from a 5-0 deficit in the final period to defeat Wayne Gretzky and the Edmonton Oilers in overtime. Not surprisingly, I was at that game, and I was one of a couple of thousand people left in the old Forum who did not leave after the second period and was able to witness Daryl's historic goal.

Even though these hockey connections gave me respite from my roller coaster show biz career, thanks to the popularity of a new TV show, I was able to see the *Ghosts of My Show Biz Past* all appear before me in one series. *The West Wing*, a contemporary political potboiler, starred Rob Lowe and featured continuing characters played by Tim Matheson and Mark Harmon! The show was extremely popular, and, as written by creator Aaron Sorkin, proved that a literate, sophisticated show could capture a broad TV audience. It really was a perfect comeback vehicle for Lowe after a rocky movie career, and the show was such a crossover hit that everybody who appeared on it received a boost, including Tim and Mark, and I was truly happy for their success.

However, sad news was about to hit all three of us Paltrow alumni, as I had gotten wind that Bruce might be sick. I gave him a call to see how he was doing, and I could not tell anything from our conversation, he sounded like the same old Bruce that we had all grown to know and love. Not long after, he passed away from lung cancer. It would not be overstating it to say that I loved Bruce like a surrogate older brother, for he was always there when you needed him to provide encouragement, advice, and moral support, albeit couched in his trademark profane, wisecracking style. The television world was devastated by this shocking news, as Bruce had touched hundreds of lives in Hollywood during his career as a producer and writer and had left a permanent legacy by giving minority actors on his shows their first breaks as directors, including Thomas Carter on *The White Shadow* and Eric Laneuville on *St. Elsewhere*. The ripple effect of overwhelming sadness amongst his friends, associates and fans was palpable, and the production company for Bruce's shows, MTM, mourned his loss. By this time Bruce's daughter, Gwyneth, had become famous in her own right as one of the brightest rising young stars in Hollywood, and it still warms my heart to remember how happy Bruce was at the Academy Awards the night that Jack Nicholson presented her with the Best Actress Oscar for *Shakespeare in Love*. My heart went out to her and her mother, actress Blythe Danner, who was cast in *Hearts of the West* right before my time at Market Street.

At that point, I was not really in touch with anybody in the movie business, so I suffered this huge loss silently with an extremely heavy heart. Within that year, I finally came up with a way to express my dedication to Bruce: I had a *In Memory* star installed at the Staples Center plaza. I felt that as the creator of *The White Shadow,* Bruce deserved to be honored at the mecca of Los Angeles basketball, the home of both the Lakers and Clippers. I was also happy to see that Bruce received an even bigger tribute—Stephen Spielberg ended his film *Catch Me if You Can* starring Tom Hanks and Leo DiCaprio with a single frame which only contained Bruce's name on it. Spielberg remained grateful to Bruce for introducing him to his wife, Kate Capshaw. I then sent Mark Harmon a Christmas card informing him of what I had done, and he not only sent me back a very personal letter of appreciation, but he also sent me a re-built A2000 baseball glove, so our baseball connection had come full circle in our shared grief. Mark then informed Blythe what I had done, and she also wrote me a very kindhearted note of appreciation. I'm sure Bruce was looking down on us from above, amused that we were trying to somehow pay tribute to him, and I vowed from that day forward to do everything I possibly could to keep his spirit alive by making sure that everybody I ever encountered would check out his classic TV shows.

Chapter 18

SON OF DEVLIN

The next few years were uneventful for me in terms of any movie business activity. I was content to dedicate myself to being the best sales executive that I could be for the Sparks, and it was an exciting time to be a Lakers' employee as well, as they were in the midst of a three-peat championship run lead by Kobe and Shaq and orchestrated by Coach Phil "guru" Jackson. I was tempted to mention to Phil in the break room that he should be appreciative of the fact that I was one of the few people in the organization that was old enough to remember him as a player, but I did not want to come off as a wise ass.

The only brief flirtation with the movie business that I had during that time was when I became friendly with one of my Sparks season seat holders, Larry Schapiro, who turned out to be a marketing executive in Paul Walker's management company. Larry's teenage daughter was a basketball player, so he made sure that she could attend our games in courtside seats, and he also footed the bill so that her team could play on the Staples Center court before some of our Sparks games. Naturally I was already familiar with Walker's work even before he hit it big in *The Fast and the Furious*, and Larry stated that he intended to bring Walker to a game at some point. When Larry also mentioned that Walker was a big Steve McQueen fan, I told him about how badly McQueen wanted to do *Nothing in Common* with Tony before his own partner pulled the plug on it. Larry wanted to see the script, so I put him in touch with Tony, but nothing ever came of it. It was too bad because I felt that the basic premise of the script could have been easily updated, but there was no fairy tale ending to this attempt on my part to get a project off the ground as a "civilian."

Not long after, however, Tony himself was back in action as he was chosen to direct a big budget action picture called *Flyboys,* based on the true story of the Lafayette Escadrille World War I flying squadron. As proof of what a small world show business really is, the producer who hired Tony was none other than Dean Devlin, the son of Don, the producer of *My Bodyguard!* This was not a family favor, however—Dean knew that Tony was a pilot and had a passion for aviation history, and simply felt that Tony was the right man for the job. Dean had already established himself as a producer to be reckoned with, having produced the smash hit Will Smith film, *Independence Day* and the well-received Mel Gibson film *The Patriot,* so *Flyboys* was going to be a big budget A list film. I was curious to see who was going to be cast in the main role as the young pilot, and I was excited to see that Tony chose James Franco. He was considered a rising young actor who was receiving a lot of word of mouth as the next big star in movies, like how Rob Lowe was talked about with *St. Elmo's Fire.* I had seen Franco in his first major role, a TV movie about James Dean, and was struck by his resemblance to the '50's icon.

Then during pre-production of the film, I was surprised to receive an e-mail from Tony, as I knew that it was an extremely busy time for him, but he wanted to let me know that Dean's co-producer, Marc Roskin, was looking for an assistant/script reader, and wanted to know if I would be interested. This was the quintessential dilemma—I had held steadfast through all the years by not taking a job as an assistant, even when I was desperate, but this one was directly connected to Tony through Dean and Tony felt that the reading aspect of the job might be right for me.

At this point, beggars couldn't be choosers, and I was extremely grateful that anybody had thought of me for anything, let alone Tony taking the time out during his own film to recommend me. I readily agreed to meet with Marc to see if there might be a fit, and we met at a local coffee shop to discuss the position. I had learned in sports ticket sales that it is important to make a "connection point" with a client, and I thought I had one with Marc. I mentioned that I had worked with Pete Weireter, the SWAT officer who had talked O.J. out of the Bronco, knowing that Marc and Dean had hired him as a technical consultant and non-speaking role in their most recent film, *Cellular*. Unfortunately, Marc responded like he had swallowed a bug—apparently Pete went a little overboard in trying to advise them on the technical details of some of the police procedures, making him a particular annoyance to Marc the production manager. Footnote on that film—it was a breakthrough role for Chris Evans, the current Captain America, and the obnoxious lawyer character in the film became the genesis for the same actor to reprise a similar character, Lewis Litt, on the current TV series *Suits*. I should have learned from my earlier meeting with David Permut not to name drop unless I was sure it was safe, but I thought it was a neat anecdote that I had worked with Pete.

Even though we hit it off well enough otherwise, I had the sinking feeling that I was once again being perceived as overqualified for the job, and similar to the Harry Gittes situation, the position itself was probably better suited to a female. Marc ultimately informed me that he needed more of the assistant aspect of the job than the reader, so he was going to go with somebody else. I lamented the fact that I was not going to be in a position to have a secondary connection to Tony again but did truly appreciate the fact that Tony was continuing to think of me. Also, Tony's assistant Karen Svobodny did her best to keep me in the loop by periodically e-mailing me a listing of job openings in the business. In the meantime, it was back to selling Sparks tickets, and I was at least consoled by the fact that I had a steady job and was still classified as a Lakers' employee.

Unbelievably, another mystical Chicago Blackhawks connection occurred during this time—one of my sales colleagues with the Sparks, Patricia Pilot, was the niece of former Blackhawks captain Pierre Pilote, and she gave me his autographed player card. Although Patricia and I had our battles over sales accounts, I was grateful for the card because it allowed me to complete a piece of framed memorabilia which included other autographs from Pilote's teammates from that era—as Citizen Kane muttered Rosebud with his dying breath, my final word will probably be "Blackhawks."

Although I did not get the Roskin job, there were soon to be a couple of other opportunities to reunite with former Market Street colleagues— the first was an anniversary screening of the Jon Voight film *Lookin' to Get Out* which was underrated during its original release despite Voight being reunited with his *Coming Home* (and *Shampoo*) director Hal Ashby. When I saw that the screening was going to be moderated by Curtis Hanson, I decided to attend the screening on the off chance that I might be able to see Curtis there and briefly reminisce about our years together at Market Street. Unbeknownst to both of us, Curtis had used an actor for *Bad Influence*, Jack Mahon, who worked in our ticket sales office for the Lakers while I was there in the early '90's, so there was that Showbiz-Showtime crossover again! Not only that, but he cast Jack again in an even bigger role in his hit film *LA Confidential*. To Curtis' credit, Jack had a physical disability, but that did not deter him from casting him. It really surprised me that even though I saw Jack in the office every day, neither of us ever spoke about our movie business connection.

I wish that I had known about the Curtis-Jack connection, because I was not sure that Curtis would even remember me. I did manage to crash the post screening reception, and sure enough Curtis was there—before I could even finish saying my name, Curtis immediately recognized me and greeted me very warmly. Not only did he remember me, but he also remembered how Hannah had hired me for the Michael Caine film *Silver Bears*, and said that Michael was there at the screening and that I should say hi to him! I didn't go that far, but I told Curtis that I honestly felt that his film *LA Confidential* was the best film of the decade, and I was relieved and heartened by the fact that Curtis had remembered me so that the Market Street dream could continue to run on in my memory bank.

Unfortunately, I was not as lucky in my next reunion attempt—there was also to be an anniversary screening of Ulu's film *Straight Time*, the film where he replaced Dustin Hoffman as the director and where I visited him on the set. I have to admit that I was very curious to find out if Ulu knew that I had recommended him for *The Deep End of the Ocean*, and was positive that he would acknowledge me if he did. While they were all doing a post film Q & A about the film, Ulu mentioned that he did not recall how they came to hire the screenwriter for *Straight Time*—I high-fived myself mentally because I did remember, and that could be the opening I needed to approach him afterward. When I did walk up to him after the Q & A and re introduced myself, my heart sank because I could tell that he did not recognize me. I should not have been surprised because thirty years had passed since our days at Market Street, but I was still heartbroken. I was able to jog his memory by reminding him that our mutual colleague at Market Street, Marian Brayton, had recommended the writer of *Straight Time*, Jeffrey Boam, based on a script of his that they had both really liked titled *All the King's Men*. Ulu did remember Marian fondly, so I walked away with the hope that he might remember me later, but I was sure that he did not know that I had recommended him for *Deep End*.

I was honestly not looking for anything from that recommendation; I just wanted him to know how much I had believed in him, and to let him know how happy I was for him that my casual conversation with Kate Guinzberg had turned into a major job for him. I continue to be consoled by the fact, however, that I consider myself one of the luckiest people in the world to have been able to work at Market Street for those five years and to have been associated with so many wonderful people during that time. It really was one of the most unique offices in the history of the movie business, and Ulu was like the kindly family uncle who also just so happened to be a genius.

Ulu passed away a few of years ago, and it remains an ongoing testament to him that his career included long standing personal relationships with some of the biggest names in the history of the business—Hoffman, De Niro, Duvall, Voight and Sheen—and that says it all about his incredible integrity and ability. I promise you that Ulu made a lasting impression on anybody he ever encountered, most of all on me.

Chapter 19

MARK HARMON FULL CIRCLE AND FULL NELSON

N ow realizing that my job opportunities in show business were going to be extremely limited at best, I decided to try and get one of my favorite books off the ground by contacting some of my remaining contacts in the business. The book was the noir-ish crime thriller that I had met with Tony about while I was reading his books but had fallen by the wayside along the way. I realized that it would take somebody with impeccable literary tastes to recognize the book's merits, as it was not written in the style of a blockbuster, so I contacted my old friendly acquaintance who had helped me through the *My Bodyguard* politics, Marianne Moloney.

Remember, Marianne was the literary agent who had submitted *Ordinary People* to Ulu, and she had since gone on to become a successful studio executive and movie producer in her own right. She produced another favorite Matt Dillon movie of mine, *Mr. Wonderful*, and I sure was glad that I had recommended Matt for *My Bodyguard*, since he went on to star in some of my all-time favorite movies! I was relieved that Marianne did not feign temporary amnesia, as some movie executives may have done when approached by a former acquaintance, but rather seemed genuinely enthusiastic to see me again. It turns out that she loved the book even more than I could have hoped for, and she was interested in pursuing it with me as a project!

Faster than you could say "Green Light," however, my momentary thrill turned into bitter disappointment. All I did was send her an e mail with some possible writer/director/actor packaging possibilities, and she fired back a dismissive reply to me that she did not believe in packaging projects but preferred to wait until a book was adapted into a script and let the literary merit speak for itself.

Therefore, she was no longer interested in pursuing the project with me and wished me luck! Of all the frequent bewildering things that happened to me during my career, this was one of the strangest, and to this day I refuse to believe that an innocent suggestion about creative possibilities deserved such a dismissive response. That uncharacteristic response continues to remain mystifying to me, and I hope that I discover one day what caused it.

Just as I was licking my wounds over that one, I received another jolt out of the blue—the Lakers were selling the Sparks, and I had no choice but to stay with the new ownership since I had so many accounts with the Sparks. Not only would I no longer be considered a Lakers employee, but the new ownership also announced that they were moving our offices out of our comfy burg of El Segundo up to the heart of downtown LA. This meant my current two-mile commute had just turned into twenty three miles one way on the most congested freeway in LA—talk about getting your world rocked. Oh, and by the way, because we are not the Lakers, we are cutting your commission in half. I thought I had survived some brutal employment changes in my career relatively well, but this was a head scratcher—earlier that year Dr. Buss had signed a ten-year extension with the league to continue to operate the team, and his previously maligned son Johnny had proven that he had what it took to be a successful sports executive. Whatever the reason, our ten-year run had come to an abrupt and baffling end, and I was honestly not sure that I could make that kind of transition at that point in my career.

Then in short order I experienced another traumatic event—while still working at the Sparks office in El Segundo, my car was T—boned while driving down the street outside our office. It was serious, and although I did see my life flash before me during impact, I did emerge relatively unscathed with some minor bumps and bruises. I did need to undergo physical therapy, however, and during that process, I experienced something even scarier—while taking a shower one morning, my heart started racing and I thought that I was having a heart attack! It turns out that I had developed panic/anxiety syndrome, and although I assumed it was caused by the accident, my Dr. told me it was due to the trauma of being forced to leave the Buss family.

I concluded that I definitely needed a change of scenery job wise, and fortunately, I still had some personal connections to the Kings hockey team so that their director of sales, Kelly Cheeseman, and their CEO of marketing, Chris McGowan, agreed to hire me as a ticket sales account executive. Then I had the strangest experience—although I had a great time selling hockey again for the next six months, I inexplicably decided that I needed to return to the Sparks. They had promoted my good friend and colleague, Pati, to sales manager, and I felt the need to not only go back and help a good friend, but I missed the rapport and family atmosphere that we had shared all those years together with the Sparks. In retrospect, it is said that panic/anxiety can adversely affect your decision-making, and that may have been the case here—I should have stayed with the team and sport I loved, but instead I returned to a chaotic situation with the Sparks with their rookie ownership and volatile management.

It turned out that Pati couldn't handle it either, so she agreed to step down shortly thereafter and return to being an account executive again. Not only that, but the Kings wound up winning their first ever championship a few years later, and if I had stayed, I would have been awarded a championship ring! I rarely look back on missed opportunities with regret, but a Kings ring would have been another fantasy come true.

This was the situation I found myself in on that fateful morning in 2008 when I received the e-mail from Mark Harmon seeking to get back in touch with me after almost five years without any contact. During that time Mark had gone to work as the lead actor on *NCIS*, a spin off on the popular TV series *JAG*, and *NCIS* had become a consistent top ten ratings hit for CBS. Naturally I quickly fired back an e-mail to Mark with all my contact information, and he called me the following morning. He told me that he was looking to develop a book wheel series character like what his rival, Tom Selleck, had done with the Jessie Stone series for CBS, and wanted to know if I would be interested in helping him find the right book series and character. Would I! Mark explained that I would be pursuing it on my own time, but if I were to find something that was eventually produced, we would be reunited as producing partners under our former Wings Productions banner. I was truly amazed at what a kind stroke of fate this turned out to be for me, ranking right up there with Mark walking into At Ease all those years ago. I eagerly accepted his proposal and enthusiastically promised him that I would get right on the case in my search for material.

Coincidentally, I had recently read a review of a book about an LA investigator, and it intrigued me because the *NY Times* reviewer stated that it contained film noir like elements in the characters and stories, so I immediately started reading the book series that it was a part of. I tipped off Mark via e-mail that I thought I was onto something, and he encouraged me to keep him updated despite his hectic production schedule with NCIS. Thus began an e-mail exchange between Mark and me that extended well over a year and may have been one of the first project pursuits conducted almost entirely by e-mail amongst all of the involved parties. It turns out that there were over a dozen books in the best-selling series, and I could tell from book one that the character of the former LAPD detective turned investigator was ideal for Mark. Much to my excitement, both Mark and his agents were enthusiastic about the character as well, but there was a fly in the ointment—the books were so popular that the film rights had been optioned in previous years, and therefore could be complicated, although none of them had been made into a movie yet. The good news was that we were seeking to make them into a TV "wheel," not individual feature films, so we embarked on the long and arduous process of trying to sort out those rights.

Along about this same time, Mark had also become a producer on *NCIS,* and his impact was immediate—the show went from being a perennial top ten show to the undisputed number one show during this same time. I was impressed but not surprised—Mark's e-mails to me were incredibly articulate, perceptive, smart, and savvy, all the qualities that make for a great producer (not to mention occasionally profanely funny as well). Not only that, but the timing of the show becoming number one certainly helped our chances of getting our project off the ground in the ultimate success begets success mentality of corporate Hollywood. While we were waiting for the rights situation to be sorted out, Mark decided that it would be a good move to try to meet with the author and pitch our version and vision of what the series could become. He then had me put together an outline and book order of which books would be the best ones for adaptation as it was unlikely that all dozen of the books would eventually be made. It took a while for their schedules to match up, but Mark and the author did eventually meet up, and word came back from the author's agent that based on meeting Mark, he was fully prepared to throw his support behind our attempt to translate his books into the TV wheel.

Once again, I was ecstatic but not surprised—as previously mentioned, Mark has an innate ability to powerfully present his viewpoint and win you over, and if he had not been an actor, he could have been a persuasive politician! Now Mark and his agents felt that they had enough ammunition to go to the head of CBS, Leslie Moonves, and express their desire for this to become Mark's special Sunday Night movie series special. When I received the e-mail that the meeting was set, I couldn't believe it—with the number one star of the number one show in television meeting with the head of the number one network, this deal could get done! Mark reported to me that the meeting had gone well and based on Mark's enthusiasm Mr. Moonves was interested in pursuing this concept on our behalf. I had to pinch myself, I might be able to emerge from the morass that the Sparks had become and fulfill my dream of becoming a producer with one of the biggest stars in television history. Armed with this newfound sense of empowerment, I started gushing to Mark via e-mail about all the talent we could line up to direct these movies, including Curtis Hanson, Ulu Grosbard, Jim Kouf and Tony Bill. I had gotten the sense that feature directors were much more open to directing TV projects, as Tony had already done, especially prestigious ones. I also told Mark how I had approached Curtis at the screening, which sparked some memories of our previous close call of working with him at Paramount.

Just when I thought the train was finally on the tracks, a bombshell hit—after Mark's agents put together a deal memo to move the project forward with the author, the author's agent overplayed his hand, and the deal was off. In the intervening weeks I tried to fill the breach with another author I liked, the one whose crime thriller I had been trying to get off the ground, but that was a bit of a reach as he would have had to come up with an original idea for a series character, and there was just not enough time. It also turned out that Mark's agents had another book series waiting in the wings (no pun intended) that Mark was going to surprise me with when a deal was made, but that project had temporarily stalled. This turn of events had drained Mark's psychic energy, and he told me that he was giving up the development chase for the time being to concentrate on *NCIS*.

As he had originally offered, Mark came through with a monetary payment for me for time spent, and his attorney (still Barry) wrote me a nice e-mail categorizing it as a loan against any future production deal income, assuring me that "that working together thing" would happen someday. Although my dream had been dashed, I really did appreciate the fact that Mark had approached me after all those years to try and continue to pursue our dream together—he was such a hot commodity that he would have had his pick of any producing partner in town, and he still chose me. It was like Tony partnering up with Ulu after the success of *The Sting*, and in the case of Mark and myself, that Bruce Paltrow bond ran deep. There is no doubt that this whole experience had whet my appetite to try and get back into the business again, so I thought that I would just come up with a dream scenario and go for it with a nothing to lose mentality.

As previously mentioned, I was a big fan of Keanu Reeves, and I knew that Tony knew that I had not jumped on his bandwagon as I had recommended Keanu to Tony for his picture, *Untamed Heart* (he went with Christian Slater instead). I then asked Tony to write a general letter of recommendation for me to Keanu's manager and producer, Erwin Stoff. Tony had recently invited me to attend a live script reading of one of his projects in development, so we were in touch, and to Tony's credit, he did write it for me. When I tried to follow up with Stoff's office, however, his secretary gave me the brush off, not because of Tony, she just didn't know who I was—I had been spoiled by Stan Kamen and his assistant Jim, who had been so accessible to me. This was ironic because I had spent most of my sports career successfully getting around these so-called gate keepers, but in this case, I just did not have the nerve to risk stepping on any toes, so I just accepted my fate and did not press the issue. However, I was determined to take one last flyer on my favorite project, the crime thriller book, so I sent one of those "if you get this" e-mails to Curtis Hanson, and much to my delighted surprise, he responded! He said that although he was in a post-production deadline on a project that he had just done for HBO (see, I was right about feature directors taking TV jobs), if I liked the book that much, that I should send it and he would read it as soon as time permits. Since I had also mentioned that I still occasionally went to our old lunch stomping grounds, Maxwell's Cafe, he asked me if it was still good. I was ecstatic that Curtis had not only replied to me but had agreed to read the book as well—that was as big as gets in this town, one of the best film directors in recent American history agreeing to read a book on my recommendation.

About a year later, I was extremely sad to hear the sobering news that Curtis had to be replaced on his most recent feature, a surfing movie called "Chasing Mavericks," due to health issues, and then was devastated to hear that he passed away a couple of years later. I consider myself extremely fortunate to have been friendly with such a kindhearted man from the Market Street era, and his generosity of spirit was a privilege to be exposed to—Curtis should be forever celebrated as one of the icons of American cinema.

In terms of Tony and Market Street I still felt that I had one piece of unfinished business left. I thought that Tony had been so thoughtful to recommend me to Marc Roskin during Flyboys that I wanted to give his partner's company, Dean Devlin and Electric Entertainment, one more shot, so I asked Tony to call Dean on my behalf. Dean promptly and cordially agreed to meet with me, and he spent a good hour of his busy schedule listening to my background and stories. I told him how I used to see him at the Beachwood Cafe at lunch while I was working for Max Goldenson, and he got a particular kick out of my *Ordinary People/My Bodyguard* story. This caused him to reflect on the synergy of how he appeared in *My Bodyguard* while both films were shooting simultaneously in Chicago, and now the star of his TV series *Leverage* starred Timothy Hutton from *Ordinary People.*

Since we were talking about Market Street, I brought up Ulu, and Dean gave me the sad news that Ulu had recently passed away. He could see that I was stunned by this news, so Dean graciously ended the meeting by offering me the opportunity to bring him any project and he would make me a producer on it if a deal were made for it.

Meeting Dean uplifted my spirits, and I am grateful to Tony for arranging it. I e-mailed Dean shortly thereafter about my crime thriller that I was determined to get made, and even though he did not usually consider books, he informed me that he would download the book immediately and would let me know if he liked it. Shortly thereafter I found out that Mark Harmon was ultimately able to get his plan B book series off the ground, *Hidden Prey* by John Sanford, with himself as producer for USA, which is the network that has the syndicated rights to *NCIS.* After it aired and received great ratings, Mark replied to my e-mail that by his own choice, there were no plans to continue the series, the one project had come together during his hiatus and he was able to do it on a one shot basis.

I also tried to recommend another book series that I thought might be right for him, but due to the ongoing success of *NCIS*, there just is not room at the inn right now. Meanwhile, the situation with the Sparks continued to deteriorate, undergoing a hostile ownership takeover, and the revolving door of presidents and mangers continued to exacerbate my anxiety.

The one positive that occurred on the Lakers side that I got a kick out of was impressive—my old sales colleague from the Lakers, Bill McDonald, had risen through the broadcasting ranks over the years and had become the television play by play announcer for the Lakers. I really did have a feeling back in the day that he would make it big, but even I did not envision that big a success story—kudos to you, Billy Mac! Also, the Lakers assistant to the head coach, Kristen Luken Brettman, did an incredibly kind thing for me in conjunction with other front office staff members of the Lakers, but she swore me to secrecy for her kind act—let's just say it fulfilled one of my lifelong dreams. Then the Sparks brought in yet another new president, and he was so abusive to us that I just couldn't take it anymore—picture Samuel L. Jackson doing the Alec Baldwin sales contest monologue from Glenn Garry, Glenn Ross, and you'll get the idea.

Fortunately, a former Sparks colleague recommended me to a sales position at USC, and I was able to seek temporary refuge there. I was motivated by the fact that former USC QB Pat Haden is the athletic director there, and I was a fan of his dating back to his days at USC (ironically, he was QB at USC while Mark was the QB at UCLA). Last Thanksgiving, I sent an e-mail to both Tony Bill and Mark Harmon wishing them a happy holiday, and they both replied immediately—both said that they had run into each other at a screening, and that my ears were burning—it was a mutual admiration society for Joe Bucz. I responded to both that it had always been my hope that they could become friends, especially since they had the bond of the Bruce Paltrow friendship. I honestly don't know why those two heavyweights of both the film and TV industry made the effort to keep in touch with me over a period of forty and thirty years respectively, but I do know the spiritual bond among the three of us was Bruce Paltrow.

Chapter 20

WHERE ARE THEY NOW?

Meridith Baer—former exploitation movie actress, tenant of Market Street and screenwriter of *Prisoners*– now owns her own enormously successful home staging company worth tens of millions of dollars. Still in touch with her via email and she is as gracious as ever.

Barbara Bell—former William Morris secretary—if anyone knows whatever happened to her, please let me know. Social media research has been fruitless.

Robert "Bobby" DeLaurentis—former contract writer for Tony Bill and close friend of Bruce Paltrow—continues long career of writing and producing TV shows, including *Fargo*.

Sam Elliott—saw him at premiere of his movie *Hero*, and he remembered me! Nominated for Academy Award for Best Supporting Actor for *A Star is Born*, but will always be known for his role of the Cowboy apparition with The Dude in *The Big Lebowski*.

Jim Kouf—writer/director friend who hit it big with *Stakeout*– segued to TV with the show *Grimm* and currently resides in Montana with producer/wife Lynn Bigelow.

Lori Loughlin—former actress of Full House whom I had lunch with at Paramount in 1989—pleaded guilty to conspiracy to commit fraud with her husband and served time in USC admissions scandal involving her two daughters.

Bill McDonald—former colleague in Forum ticket sales office is still the TV play by play voice of the LA Lakers.

Bob Miller—former voice of the LA Kings hockey team—finally won his championship ring and retired for health reasons.

Pam Shriver—former Forum sales assistant—her daughter Stacia married and divorced Chad McQueen, son of Steve. Stacia is now married to Luc Robitaille, former Kings hockey star and current Kings president.

Tim Sullivan—former At Ease security agent and LA Kings Account Executive—successful commercial real estate agent and family man.

Alan Swyer—former screenwriter of *The Buddy Holly Story*, has made boxing documentaries and written a novel, *The Beard*. Reconnected with him through our mutual friend, boxing announcer Jim FitzGerald.

RIP

In the ruthless milieu of the LA grind, these wonderful gentlemen all somehow found the time to help a young man climb the ladder, and, more importantly, help him after he fell off—may they rest in peace:

Jerry Bick, Film Noir producer

Jerry Buss, owner of LA Lakers

Ulu Grosbard, stage and film director

Curtis Hanson, film director, writer and producer

Stan Kamen, Film and TV agent

Bruce Paltrow, TV producer

Fred St. Francis (Stankas), Forum sales manager

Tim Wood, manager for Rob Lowe

Bob Wunsch, literary agent and producer of "Slap Shot"

ABOUT THE AUTHOR

Joe Bucz is currently an Account Executive with the Los Angeles Lakers, "he still calls strangers and asks them for money (Wall Street)"

www.ingramcontent.com/pod-product-compliance
Lightning Source LLC
Chambersburg PA
CBHW071355120626
46546CB00002B/704